The Many Faces of Abuse

Treating the Emotional Abuse of High-Functioning Women

by
Joan Lachkar, Ph.D.

A JASON ARONSON BOOK

ROWMAN & LITTLEFIELD PUBLISHERS, INC.
Lanham • Boulder • New York • Toronto • Oxford

A JASON ARONSON BOOK

ROWMAN & LITTLEFIELD PUBLISHERS, INC.

Published in the United States of America
by Rowman & Littlefield Publishers, Inc.
A wholly owned subsidary of The Rowman & Littlefield Publishing Group, Inc.
4501 Forbes Boulevard, Suite 200, Lanham, Maryland 20706
www.rowmanlittlefield.com

PO Box 317
Oxford
OX2 9RU, UK

British Library Cataloguing in Publication Information Available

Library of Congress Cataloging-in-Publication Data

Lachkar, Joan.
    The many faces of abuse : treating the emotional abuse of
high-functioning women / by Joan Lachkar.
        p. cm.
    Includes bibliographical references and index.
    ISBN 0-7657-0065-4 (alk. paper)
    1. Psychological abuse. 2. Psychologically abused women.
3. Abusive men. 4. Personality disorders. 5. Marital
psychotherapy. I. Title.
RC569.5.P75L33 1997
616.85'822—dc21   95-53035

Printed in the United States of America

⊖™ The paper used in this publication meets the minimum requirements of American
National Standard for Information Sciences—Permanence of Paper for Printed Library
Materials, ANSI/NISO Z39.48-1992.

To Peter

with love

Contents

Acknowledgments

The stimuli for writing this book were my participation in the human rights movement, my interest in psychohistory, and my clinical practice. My active involvement as newsletter editor of the Walter Briehl Human Rights Foundation alerted me to the special treatment needs of victims of human rights violations, and many of my patients provided me with insights that victims of abuse also need special treatment. At the Walter Briehl Human Rights Foundation, I have fond memories of working with Elyse and the late Alexander Rogawsky, Grace and the late Samuel Eisenstein, S. L. Pomer, Shirley Magidson, Marvin Osman, Harvey Weintraub, and of course Marie Briehl. I wish to express special tribute to Dr. Inge Kemp Genefke, the founding medical director of the International Rehabilitation and Research Center for Torture Victims in Copenhagen, the first such center in the world.

It was not easy to write a book of this nature. Without the support of my mentors, colleagues, supervisees, students, friends, and family (my daughters Sharon, Pamela, and Nicole), my publisher, and my patients, this book would not have been possible. I am grateful to all those who encouraged me to investigate this highly sensitive topic. I wish to pay a special tribute to my mother, Sally Berke, who passed away while this book was being written, always remembering her words, "You can do it!"

I shall always be indebted to my mentors in the psychoanalytic adventure: James Grotstein, Frederick Vaquer, and Albert Mason, for their exquisite supervision and explication of complex analytic theory. I owe much to Otto Kernberg, whose work on aggression and perversion has influenced my own thoughts and theories.

Particularly stimulating were my colleagues in the area where psychology and psychoanalysis intersect with history, anthropology, and other social sciences and humanities: Peter Loewenberg, psychohistorian and psychoanalyst, Lloyd deMause, editor of the *Journal of Psychohistory* for his encouragement to extend my work beyond psychotherapy and marital relations, and Peter Berton, specialist in international relations and research psychoanalyst, who guided me in the cross-cultural areas.

In this book, as well as in my previous book on narcissistic/borderline couples, my concept of "the dance," the pas de deux between two anguished partners, grew out of my lifelong obsession with dance and classical ballet. I salute my teachers, the late ballet master Carmelita Maracci, Stanley Holden, and fellow dancers.

The publication of this book was greatly facilitated by the Jason Aronson, Inc. staff: Michael Moskowitz (publisher), Norma Pomerantz (director of author relations), Judy Cohen (production editor), and especially Michael Gorkin, who helped edit the final draft. It is a pleasure to acknowledge the enthusiasm of Dr. Jason Aronson for my work and his patience and empathic understanding, especially when I went beyond my deadlines.

A special thanks is due to the librarians at the Los Angeles Psychoanalytic Society/Institute (LAPSI), the Southern California Psychoanalytic Institute, the library of the Neuropsychiatric Institute and the Biomedical Library at UCLA, and to my research assistants Amanda and Rob Greenhalgh, Titi Li, Jonah Minton, and my daughter Nicole.

I salute Robert Geffner, President of the Family Violence and Sexual Assault Institute, and Robbie Rossman, of the University of Denver, for inaugurating and co-editing a new publication, *The Journal of Emotional Abuse: Interventions, Research, and Theories of Psychological Maltreatment, Trauma, and Nonphysical Aggression* and thank them for inviting me to serve on its editorial board.

But perhaps most valuable have been the contributions from my colleagues (Eve Kahr, Hindy Nobler, Orli Peter, Ellie Pynes, Stephen Rush, Janet Smith, and

Shelley Ventura); the graduate students, mental health professionals, and all others who have attended my workshops, seminars, and conference presentations; and my supervisees, whose challenges, questions, and contributions have sharpened my understanding of this important topic.

I have left for last that group to whom I am most indebted: my patients, who have struggled through many difficult times in their relationships, but have borne with the work, have not given up, and have come to love the beauty of psychoanalytic psychotherapy work. Their anguish, frustration, and pain have taught me the pervasive meaning of the forces that drive many victims into inseparable bondage. My patients have added that crucial experiential dimension that brings to life the drama of emotional abuse.

Introduction

A vulture was hacking at my feet. It had already torn my boots and stockings to shreds, now it was hacking at the feet themselves. Again and again it struck at them, then circled several times restlessly. around me, then returned to continue its work. A gentleman passed by, looked on for a while, then asked me why I suffered the vulture. "I'm helpless," I said. "When it came and began to attack me, I of course tried to drive it away, even to strangle it, but these animals are very strong, it was about to spring at my face, but I preferred to sacrifice my feet. Now they are almost torn to bits."

"The Vulture," Franz Kafka (1935)

The plight of the emotionally abused women is captured well by Franz Kafka. The demise of the victim is like the dalliance between vulture and prey. The vulture eats away slowly at the still living body, sucking the blood of its victim. The abuser, just as slowly, eats away at a woman's self-esteem, and while he does so, he sucks the lifeblood of her selfhood, painfully diminishing, then devouring it. The victim/prey, not knowing how to free herself of the abuser/vulture, allows the bird to claw and peck away at her.

Despite the compelling nature of this plight, we, as a society, often dismiss or ignore the emotionally abused woman, particularly the high-functioning abused woman. We are made uncomfortable by "victims," especially if we think they may be responsible in some way for the abuse. We tend not to think of emotional abuse as real abuse, that which results in blackened eyes, shattered ear drums, or broken limbs. Unfortunately, what we do not appreciate is that emotional abuse can break our spirits and our souls.

We show little or no empathy for the high-functioning woman who is abused. Whether she is a doctor, a corporate executive, a professor, an entrepreneur, or a psychologist, we chastise her with, "You, a professional! How could a woman like you put up with being abused? You're independent, you make a good living. Just leave!" With all her capacities, skills, and education, we believe she should know better. Why? Because we view her as privileged. And with privilege comes the burden of keeping up appearances, of not challenging the status quo, and, ultimately, of not complaining. We too often overlook the fact that along with this high-functioning side, there is an undeveloped, thwarted side; that behind the competence, there may be a vulnerable and needy person.

WHY THIS BOOK IS IMPORTANT

The world of psychotherapy is witnessing an onslaught of literature on physical abuse that has reached unprecedented levels. There has been a near saturation on this subject, including books on violence against children, on incest, and on spousal battering. Yet, the incidence of abuse continues to increase. The battered wife syndrome, the most obvious and the most common form of abuse, has generated a plethora of books (deMause 1974, Dutton 1995, Hoffman 1981, Painter 1985, Rosenbaum and O'Leary 1981, Straus 1980, Walker 1984a,b). According to the United States Department of Justice, more than 2 ½ million women experience violence annually. Nearly two in three women who are the victims of violence are related to or know their abusers. Although women are found to be significantly less likely to become victims of violent crime, they are more vulnerable to particular types of perpetrators. Whereas men are more likely to be victimized by acquaintances or strangers, women are just as likely to be victimized by intimates, such as husbands or boyfriends, as they are by acquaintances or strangers. The rate of victimization by intimates is nearly ten times greater for females than for males. On the average each year, women experience 572,032 violent victimizations at the hands of intimates, compared to 48,983 incidents committed against men. Among women who experience a violent victimization, injuries occur almost twice as frequently when the offender is an intimate (59%) rather than a stranger (27%). Injured women are also more likely to require medical care if the attacker is an intimate (27%) rather than a stranger

(14%). Six times as many women victimized by intimates (18%) as those victimized by strangers (3%) do not report their violent victimization to police because they fear reprisal from the offender (Bachman 1994).

Approximately one-third of the men counseled (for battering) are professionals who are well respected in their jobs and communities. They include doctors, lawyers, ministers, and business executives. Women of all cultures, races, occupations, income levels, and ages are battered by husbands, boyfriends, lovers, and partners.

When a woman is sexually harassed or physically abused, she has some rights and some legal recourse, but when she is emotionally abused, that recourse is generally undermined.

Emotional abuse has been relatively neglected as a subject of psychological research and writing at the very time that clinicians are witnessing an increase in the number of individuals suffering from various forms of emotional violation. Emotional abuse has also received far less notoriety in the public forum than has physical abuse. When emotional abuse takes place, the police may or may not respond and, to date, there is no legal recourse for the emotionally abused. When such abuse occurs against women who have prominent careers, there is a sinister backlash. The abuse is too shameful to admit. When a high-functioning woman does admit it, she is either not believed or is ridiculed: "What! You, an attorney, and you're abused? Yeah, right," or "You're a doctor. What's a woman like you doing with a man like that?"

This book focuses on the emotional abuse of high-functioning women, its devastating effects, and the helplessness these women feel when sucked into the quagmire of its grip. Victims of psychological abuse often react in ways that prove to be as debilitating as the abuse itself: withdrawal, hopelessness, guilt, shame, and psychosomatic illness, to name just a few. Moreover, we have not had, until now, a clear definition of what constitutes emotional abuse or therapeutic guidelines for acknowledging the unique problems that occur in the treatment of the emotionally abused high-functioning woman. This psychodynamic approach is the heart of this book.

LITERATURE REVIEW

Many authors have written about physical abuse, but while they make references to emotional abuse, very little has been written specifically on psychological or emotional abuse. As a subject of psychological research, this form of abuse has been relatively neglected. Most researchers or analysts explore issues of aggression, perversion, sadism, masochism, hostility, rage, and acting out, but they do not speak directly to the abuse. Others may adhere to more cognitive or behavioral approaches, how-to, or quick fix methods, which run the risk of oversimplification, tend to blame the victim, ignore the abuser's aggression, and do not take into account the interaction between the perpetrator and the victim. Furthermore, few authors have approached this topic from a psychodynamic perspective. Regardless of the clinician's particular theoretical orientation, most practitioners who treat sufferers or survivors find that patients have great difficulty breaking away from their abusive attachments. Emotional abuse is not obvious, and the resistances that come into play become nearly impenetrable as we attempt to recognize and treat the patient (Lachkar, in press).

Loring (1994) breaks new ground in describing both overt and covert emotional abuse and makes crucial linkages to other types of abuse. Dutton (1995) provides extensive research on the battered woman syndrome suffered by victims of both physical and psychological abuse. He explores the dynamics of the victim/abuser relationship, and notes the borderline personality organization as the one most inclined toward violence or abuse. He introduces the concept of "traumatic bonding," which is similar to what Loring has referred to as "intermittent reinforcement" (messages alternate between positive and negative).

THE ETIOLOGY OF EMOTIONAL ABUSE

The Many Faces of Abuse examines emotional abuse from both intrapsychic and interpersonal perspectives, since the intricate nature of emotional abuse makes it impossible to separate internal and relational worlds. Concepts abstracted from classical psychoanalysis, self psychology, group psychology, and above all, object relations theory, help delineate the unconscious dynamics of emotional abuse. From these theories the interactive dynamics of treating abuse are drawn. The effort here is to help therapists understand and diagnose women who have been emotionally abused.

How can we hope to understand the nature of emotional abuse? "Dual projective identification" (Lachkar 1992) is a concept I have employed to describe how both partners project back and forth and identify with different aspects of the self. Through the analysis of the partners' mutual cycles of projections and identifications, we have a better chance to perceive how one projects a negative feeling into the other and how the other (the victim) identifies with what is being projected.[1] We then have an opportunity to examine why the

---

1. I employ the preposition *into* and not *onto* to convey that in projective identification the individual employing this defense (1) in fantasy imagines extruding a part of self or introject and depositing it *in* another, and (2) through his or her actual behavior attempts to induce *in* the other the experience of being that extruded part. Generally, projective identification cycles take place outside the awareness of both individuals—the projector and the recipient of the projection—and, indeed, much of the therapeutic work involves making the partners aware of how this process goes on between them.

woman absorbs such negative projections. Furthermore, I have found that the partners share an unconscious fantasy, one that becomes enacted repeatedly within the interpersonal dyad. This is the bitter paradox found at the heart of dual projective identification: the partner who is loved and adored is also the partner who is felt to be the bitter enemy, the target of aggression and hatred. The intimate partner who is abusive is the same one who provides hope, love, caring, validation, and intimacy. This partner is, transferentially, the parent who is both loved and hated. The abused intimate partner who wants to be loved identifies with the projections (of the abusing partner), and in so doing she feels demeaned, ridiculed, controlled, and emotionally scapegoated. In object-relational terms this is known as splitting of the object, especially when the conflicts inherent within this paradox become highly eroticized and sexualized. In self psychological terms this is known as the idealized object (one who can do no wrong). This is the odd-couple relationship of an all-encompassing mother of responsibility bonded to a painful internal object, or, as Sheldon Bach so succinctly calls it, the "mother of pain" (1994, p. 14). Behind the armor of the high-functioning woman, there is a little girl in hiding who has lost contact with the self by denying dependency needs and overvaluing the other.

Robert Lifton (1986), in *Nazi Doctors*, refers to this kind of splitting as "doubling," a notion he applied to the

Nazis. The German murderers who committed horrific crimes during the day were the same Germans who in the evening would return home to their families as loving and kind husbands and fathers. We can see this same paradox enacted by the abusive parent who both loves and hates his or her child, who is alternately caring and hurtful. An emotional abuser often takes on the role of this early, internalized parent. Thus, it is common for abusive adults to project the victimized part of themselves into their partners and, through the abuse, enact the behavior of their own aggressively sadistic or aggressively depriving parents who, at other times, behaved in loving ways. The abused partner then is induced to feel as the abuser did as a child with the aggressive, depriving parents.

While the primary emphasis in this book is on women, much of what is said also can be applied to men who are abused. More often it is the wives who fall prey to this psychological domination. However, I have chosen to focus on abused high-functioning women for two reasons. First, as we have seen statistically, abuse is far more often directed at women than at men. Second, as we have seen anecdotally, these particular women are seldom envisioned as the kind of women who would be the recipients of, or allow, such abuse.

In my practice, I treat many professional women who feel on top of the world at work, only to return home to become diminished to a state of helplessness and victimization. It is difficult for these women to face up to their emotional abuse; they feel responsible for the attacks and deserving of them. When we think of abuse, we tend to think of a stereotypical image, a bully or a violent man frantically chasing an innocent female victim. Unless one is brutally beaten, raped, or assaulted, it is difficult for most women to face up to abuse, or even to recognize it.

The dynamic relationship between the perpetrator and the victim is depicted in this book as a "dance": the dance between the abuser and the abused. The metaphor of a dance brings clearly to mind the notion of dual projective identification. The destructive choreography of projected fantasies is staged and restaged, evoking in the perpetrator powerful, vengeful, aggressive feelings, and, in the victim, powerlessness, shame, and guilt.

The main focus of this book is a delineation of the dance of emotional abuse, making clear the distinctions between physical and emotional abuse. Here, emotional abuse is treated as a separate entity, because unlike physical abuse, which is overt and cyclical in nature, emotional abuse is both overt and covert, and is continuous and insidious. Victims of emotional abuse, unlike their physically abused counterparts, may be unaware of previous violations and often are unable to recognize that they, in fact, are currently being abused (Loring 1994).

TYPOLOGY OF EMOTIONAL ABUSE:
DIAGNOSTIC DISTINCTIONS

As we explore the many faces of abuse, we will discover that there are probably as many variations of abuse as there are abusers and victims. How then can we comprehend what the men and women in these emotionally abusive relationships cannot? By grasping the emotional life of both abuser and abused and the magnetic pull between them, we can reach an understanding of what constitutes emotional abuse; we can see how each partner has his and her own idiosyncratic nature as well as his and her propensity for shaping different forms of relational bonds. In this effort, I will define five different kinds of male abusers within specific diagnostic categories (drawn from *DSM-IV*) in order to focus on the typology and description of the women who stay with these men. For each of the five types—the narcissistic abuser, the borderline abuser, the passive-aggressive abuser, the obsessive-compulsive abuser, and the schizoid abuser—we will examine: (1) the nature of the disorder, (2) the defenses employed, (3) the typology of women involved and their diagnostic distinctions, (4) how the "dance" of emotional abuse is played out in accord with the couple's desire for intimate attachment, (5) case illustrations, and (6) treatment suggestions. Through this depiction, we will see how the unconscious collusion of the couple leads to agonizing emotional torment for both partners and how therapeutic techniques can begin to intervene in this collusion.

In neurotic and characterological relationships, there exist distinct differences in how each partner experiences the shortcomings of the other as abuse (real and/or fantasized), and how these shortcomings can activate, accentuate, or contribute to the combative nature of the couple. It is crucial to understand the state of mind shared in destructive mutuality by the perpetrator and the victim of the abuse in order to provide a specific treatment modality. Case histories and clinical illustrations are provided to reflect the variations of primitive attachments between high-functioning women and the men to whom they are drawn, along with various treatment approaches designed to effectuate corrective emotional experiences.

As we examine the five categories of abusers, we will notice that there are common themes played out to some degree or another by each type of couple: (1) an indifference toward the partner's suffering; (2) an intolerance of dependency needs of both self and other, as well as of frustration and of criticism, which, in turn, gets expressed by exerting control over the partner, withholding from the partner, and non-validation of the partner's experience; and (3) a grandiose sense of entitlement characterized by withdrawal, unavailability, and aloofness. Characterological traits, behaviors, and archaic conflicts are explored within the five specific diagnostic categories in order to understand couples' underlying defenses (most prevalent among them splitting and projection).

IS ABUSE MORE PERVASIVE TODAY?

Abuse and men's aggression toward women have been prevalent throughout history. Today we are seeing a variation of the same virulent "virus," but our understanding of the phenomenon has not grown sufficiently. Interpersonal conflicts are not simple, for they are composed of many complex facets (control, domination, sadism, envy, jealousy, hatred, greed, and dependency). To arrive at an in-depth understanding of such longstanding conflicts between men and women, we need to examine the problems from both the societal and interpersonal dimensions.

From the societal point of view we might ask to what extent have economic growth, wealth, and the rise of the women's movement impacted women's lives. We have become a narcissistic, materialistic, "me" society that supports grandiose delusional fantasies rather than commitment to kinship and family ties. We might say that we are living in an era where entitlements are like an open-ended bank account. Perhaps we are all products of a rapidly changing culture whose values are status, fame and fortune, and self-involvement. Other influences include the breakdown of the family and community, the rising divorce rates, delayed marriages, and single mothers. Consider that among white women, the percentage of single mothers has more than doubled in the past decade. Among women with managerial jobs or professional careers, it has almost tripled. The percentage of children living in single-mother households has tripled (Peace at Home 1997).

Many women have achieved the American Dream, a lifestyle many others envy. From the interpersonal perspective, this creates greater expectations and more responsibilities. President Clinton has appointed many women to cabinet positions and as heads of sub-cabinet agencies. The expansion of women's occupational opportunities has contributed significantly to the shifting of power in society more toward women. Yet as desirable as this may appear, new pressures and problems emerge, including feelings of isolation and abandonment. One would also think that with the advent of the women's movement, and the ever-increasing roles of women, aggression and hostilities toward them would diminish, but such is not the case. In the past, when the woman was the victim, she was denigrated for her weakness and was oppressed; now when she becomes assertive and powerful, she becomes the target of man's competitive and rivalrous nature, and thus subject to even more aggression and abuse. Do men, consciously or not, project their hostility onto the women who usurped their positions? Additionally, with the rapid financial independence of women and the relatively low level of involvement of male partners in child-rearing and housework, there has been a significant decrease in marriage benefits for women.

In spite of some feminist claims that men are dispensable and that women can perform the dual roles of mother and father and can substitute for the man's role à la Murphy Brown, a Rand Corporation report (DaVanzo and Rahman 1993) states that marriage and the presence of strong family ties and kinship improve health and survival, and that the currently married have significantly better health and longevity than non-married single-parent peers.

In the face of overwhelming problems confronting our society, can we afford to care about seemingly privileged, high-functioning women who many believe allow themselves to be abused? The answer is not only "yes," but if we can begin to understand this group of women, we may arrive at some universal laws that govern or concern all women. Although societal attitudes toward women certainly do play a vital role, we must be able to determine the connections all women share from an intrapsychic, developmental, and interpersonal perspective, and thus determine the roots of emotional abuse.

HOW THIS BOOK CAME ABOUT

My interest in pain, abuse, and conflict in marital relations was a direct outcome of my research in psychohistory, as well as my participation in the human rights movement. In "The Arab-Israeli Conflict" (Lachkar 1983) and subsequent writings, I suggested that two specific myths, based on recurring themes in the Bible and the Koran, had significant influence in perpetuating that conflict. The first is the belief that Jews are God's "chosen people," and second, that the Arabs are an "orphan" society, the abandoned child of God. Deriving from these mythic origins are hurts and injuries deeply rooted in age-old sentiments that continually resurface and give rise to many shared collective group fantasies. In the Middle East, contention is not only over land and occupied territories, but over betrayal, dependency, entitlement, oedipal rivals, emotional boundaries, preservation of self, and group identity. Translated at the unconscious level, marital partners are not really battling over sex, money, custody, children (external events), but over love, intimacy, dependency, abandonment, specialness, and issues of power and control. I began to conceive of Arabs and Jews as a metaphor for the narcissistic/ borderline couple. Exploring Middle Eastern psychology, mythology, and religion, I began to see a dynamic relationship similar to that of couples I was treating in my clinical practice. I found that these myths and ideologies could foster in various men an identification with leaders who exhibit aggressive attitudes toward, and inflict sadistic assaults upon, women. In other words, I began to notice parallels between political and marital conflicts. The result was my first book, *The Narcissistic/Borderline Couple: A Psychoanalytic Perspective on Marital Treatment* (1992).

In examining a variety of couples with narcissistic, borderline, and other personality organizations, I saw that many of the patients I treated were high-functioning corporate executives, and I wondered how they could so rapidly regress. Many of these women were not physically violated, but were emotionally abused. I began to focus on emotional abuse of high-functioning women. I also realized that there are other types of abusers and many different venues of aggression. I therefore expanded my focus on the range of abusers to include the passive-aggressive, the obsessive-compulsive, and the schizoid. This led to a typology of women who choose to stay with their abusers. As more and more cross-cultural couples are filling our consultation rooms, I began to question the cultural and gender-related differences and generally the vicissitudes of men's aggression against women. Can we determine some universal laws that are psychologically applicable to the treatment of abused high-functioning women? Where do the boundaries between acts of cruelty and cultural tradition interface?

DEFINING EMOTIONAL ABUSE

Can we define emotional abuse? Peace at Home, Inc. (1997) publishes a warning list, indicating the danger signs of emotional abuse (see Chapter 1). For example, it suggests that it is emotionally abusive to betray trust, misuse authority, always claim to be right, not listen or respond to the needs of the other, interfere with the work of the other, engage in economic control, or manipulate or withhold money. Although helpful, these guidelines do not address the intrapsychic needs and vulnerabilities, the culturally influenced dynamics, and the unconscious motivations emerging between the partners, nor do they show how each partner either consciously or unconsciously contributes to the abuse as s/he searches for some way to meet archaic needs. Until now, we have not had a clear definition of what constitutes emotional abuse or therapeutic guidelines for treating the distinct problems that occur in the high-functioning woman who is emotionally abused. Emotional abuse is an ongoing process and differs from physical abuse in that one person consciously or unconsciously attempts to destroy the will, needs, desires, or perceptions of another. Normal couples will from time to time "abuse" each other, but emotional abuse has an undercurrent of hostility. According to Loring (1994), the most salient feature of emotional abuse is its insidious nature. It is continual and operates at two levels: overtly and covertly. Overt abuse is openly demeaning (verbal remarks, put-downs, constant criticisms). Covert abuse is more subtle and insidious, but no less devastating, and it creates in the victim confusion, chaos, uncertainty, and insecurity (Loring 1994).

DIFFERENCE BETWEEN PHYSICAL AND EMOTIONAL ABUSE

Emotional abuse is closely allied to physical abuse, but nonetheless should be distinguished from the latter. One major difference is in the timing. Physical abuse is cyclical, occurring on and off, whereas emotional abuse is insidious and omnipresent (Loring 1994).

Studies suggest that emotional abuse can be just as devastating as physical abuse, and in some cases even more so (Follingstad et al. 1990, Loring 1994, Walker 1984a,b). Another difference is that many women who stay in emotionally abusive relationships do not necessarily report a prior history of abuse (Loring 1994).

Walker (1984a,b), Dutton (1995), Loring (1994), and Straus (1980) have described physical abuse as an uncontrollable destructive act and lack of responsiveness to cues from the victim. They note such outstanding features as escalating violence to the point of uncontrollable rage, which subsides only when the aggressor is exhausted.

In the following chapters, we will explore the nature

and conflicts of the high-functioning woman as we examine in depth those primitive aspects of her psyche that ensnare her in the vicious cycle of emotional abuse. In doing so, we will investigate the influence of gender identification as well as various cultural factors. As we focus on five types of male abusers and the women who stay with them, we will discover the intrapsychic and relational forces that bind them in the throes of the dance between abuser and abused. We will discuss the pivotal contributions of such theorists as Sigmund Freud, Melanie Klein, W. R. D. Fairbairn, Donald Winnicott, Otto Kernberg, Wilfred Bion, and Heinz Kohut, in order to see how both intrapsychic and interpersonal approaches are useful in understanding and treating emotional abuse, especially as it occurs with high-functioning women.

In order to meet the treatment needs of high-functioning women (as well as all victims of emotional abuse), we must commit ourselves to an in-depth understanding of the mysterious forces that lead to such abuse. Women who are abused need to know that they are not responsible for the underlying causes of the abuse they suffer, nor are they deserving of it. But they also need to recognize their unconscious participation in the abuse, and learn that they do not have to remain victims. To accomplish this shift, therapists, victims, and perpetrators alike need to be aware of the "dance" between abuser and abused. Further, therapists need to be schooled in those treatment techniques that can transform the hatred and pain that fuel emotional abuse in order to effect a new emotional experience. It is my hope that this book will provide the clear understanding for which professionals have searched as they treat the emotionally abused.

1

High-Functioning Women and Emotional Abuse

Deanna, a 34-year-old professional woman, goes to a department store with Greg, her controlling, obsessive-compulsive husband, to return a pair of shoes. He extorts a promise from her that she will not shop, and to ensure this promise he holds onto her purse. On her way out, she feels compelled to look at some jewelry. Glancing at his watch, her husband becomes angry as he is kept waiting. Convinced that Deanna has broken her promise, he impatiently strides through the various departments, first the shoes, the cosmetics, then the jewelry. When he glimpses his wife standing at the display counter, he becomes incensed at her failure to keep her word. Deciding to "teach her a lesson," he storms out of the store, abandoning her.

Deanna looks up to see her husband leaving. She rushes after him, calling his name with endless apologies, begging him to wait. He dashes ahead of her and drives away, while she stands, feeling forsaken and shamed, with no purse, no money, and no way to get home.

Too humiliated to return to the store, Deanna searches for a pay phone, using her calling card number to call one friend after another trying to find a ride. No one answers. Finally, she calls a cab. Back at her house, she asks the cab driver to wait while she asks her husband for money to pay the fare. Opening the door, Greg casts a long, unwavering look at Deanna, then yells, "Bitch!" and slams the door in her face.

Deanna runs next door to a neighbor who offers her the cab fare and a place to stay until Greg calms down. As the young woman pays the driver, he says, "Gee Miss, you need some help. I think you and your husband ought to get some therapy." Deanna sighs, "You're right. The irony is, I am a therapist!"

Deanna is typical of many high-functioning women. Indeed, with her Ph.D. in clinical psychology, a thriving therapeutic practice, her home in an upscale neighborhood, and three supposedly model children, she seems the quintessential woman who "has it all." But, of course, there is another side to this image: a woman who is embedded in a volatile relationship, and who suffers from a lack of a secure sense of self. She needs external objects to shore up her wounded, non-cohesive self. And yet, at first glance she seems like a high-functioning woman. Why?

DEFINING THE HIGH-FUNCTIONING WOMAN

The high-functioning woman's (HFW) external life reveals a highly motivated, energetic, well-educated, and career-oriented woman using many creative capacities to achieve status and become successful according to our society's standards of material success. However, the term *high functioning*, is not defined solely by level of education, occupation, and status, but also needs to be measured by the individual's psychological defense structures. In her work, she may be decisive, comfortable with her autonomy, and extremely competent in the fulfillment of her decisions and responsibilities, but in her psychic life she may operate at many different levels of ego functioning. High-functioning women's personalities can operate on different tracks, can vacillate from momentary states of wholeness, autonomy, and independence to fragmentation and helplessness.

I have divided the high-functioning woman into two categories; the higher level HFW and the lower level HFW.[1] The level of functioning depends on the nature of the person's defensive mechanisms (above all, the use of splitting) as well as the degree of impulse control, acting out, and addictive or compulsive behaviors. The higher level woman operates at a more advanced level of superego functioning and is dominated by guilt and depressive anxieties. In a higher level or psychologically healthier woman, reality testing offers relief, judgment is not readily obscured, and the woman is less likely to identify with the abuse or the negative projections (Lachkar 1992). The lower level HFW operates at a more

---

1. These categories have been inspired by Melanie Klein's two major contributions, the paranoid-schizoid position and the depressive position (Klein 1957), as two important phases the infant moves through during development.

primitive level of superego functioning, which is perse-cutory in nature. She exhibits shame/blame defenses and is dominated by envy, magical thinking, and perse-cutory anxieties. The lower level HFW has often been exposed to traumatic experiences and is prone to pre-oedipal conflicts. For her, reality testing does *not* offer relief; it is replaced by infantile functioning and the loss of self (Vaquer 1991). She continues to berate or perse-cute herself, fantasizing that everything is her fault.

In Winnicott's (1965) terms, the high-functioning woman may be viewed as one who has a highly devel-oped "false self." In other words, early in life, this woman developed a defensive organization to protect or insulate her "true self," a self that was either intruded upon or neglected by her early caregivers. Insulated by this socially appropriate false self, she is able to master her concrete world, while her subjective world—her true self—remains vulnerable to nameless fears and unful-filled yearnings. In short, there is a dichotomy between her resourceful, competent, and usually successful outer self and her needy, deprived, and harmed inner self. The internal world of the HFW is not imbued with confidence and creative energy; instead, she is tormented with unbearable shame and guilt, and inner chaos. While high functioning in certain arenas of life, she struggles with unresolved and intense infantile conflicts, needs, and longings. At the intrapsychic and interrelational level, she is psychologically primitive.

What do I mean by "primitive"? The personality structures of these women are determined not by healthy and progressive development but by the defensive mechanisms they have had to develop in order to survive psychically. Early defenses, such as splitting, projection, projective identification, omnipotent denial, and magical thinking play out in these adult women's reactions to emotional experiences. By way of example, let us look at the high-functioning woman who operates from the early paranoid-schizoid position. In this position, unwanted and threatening parts of the self are evacuated and projected into the object. While this projection is made up of unconscious fantasies, the psychic material nonetheless is experienced as real and concrete to the individual. Women who live within this paranoid schizoid position tend to choreograph their outer experience to match their psychic experience. One woman might feel, "All men are cruel and destructive." Another might give up, believing, "I already know what he'll say. Nothing will make any difference." Yet another may contend, "I'm helpless; he's stronger than I am." Still another may engage in magical thinking, a form of projective identification that the other should know what she needs without her having to tell him.

In their intimate, emotionally abusive relationships, these women confuse love with pain. As the object is idealized, it also becomes eroticized. Struggling to survive within their psychic space with idealized partners, these women attempt to counter their anxiety by becoming demanding, controlling, and/or clingy. Even though they may appear polished and stable in their working environments, they live with an almost unbearable sense of need, inadequacy, and humiliation. Understanding this, we can then comprehend why intelligent, well-educated women who are accomplished in their professional lives can be drawn to powerful, controlling men who give the appearance of caretaking and strength.

Such women conceive of themselves as worthwhile only when they are providing a function for others, such as sex or money, time or attention. While false-self organizations offer a kind of protection from perceived psychic danger, they exact the requirement that the bearer must remain in psychic denial of pain, stress, and unfulfillment. Oftentimes, the result of such denial is that other people do not take their problems seriously. High-functioning women find themselves treated as they are viewed: as the controlling woman, the phallic/erotic woman, the passive/submissive woman, the hungry/insatiable woman, the co-dependent woman, or the blaming/attacking woman. In the end, they are usually left feeling even more deprived and empty, seldom experiencing gratification in their most significant relationships.

Generally, abused high-functioning women do not have healthy superegos to guide them in choices, boundary setting, and behavior. At the more highly developed level, their superegos are simply harsh; at the lower level, their superegos are downright persecutory. The language of the superego speaks through their bodies; their early life experiences, which were stored as body memories, get triggered by their abusive partners. As this early psychic material is processed through their bodies they experience any number of physical complaints—headaches, asthma, gastrointestinal difficulties, twitching, restlessness, and hair pulling or nail biting.

Many of these women, have a "reverse superego," a term I use to capture this process of aligning oneself with the negative aspects of the superego through identification. More recently, I have extended this notion to "reverse love": opposition love or love that moves in a negative direction. When the superego loses its original function as a moral guide, it is transformed into either a negative or neglectful one. In healthy development, the guiding superego holds the voice of the father/authority, reminding the child of her accomplishments. In unhealthy development, the reverse superego holds the judgment that even when the child is good or works hard, she does not deserve recognition or rewards. This reverse superego becomes replicated in the abusive partner of the high-functioning woman. Certain women, like the obsessive, the hysteric, and the narcissistic, will be able to tolerate better the anxiety they feel in reaction to this reverse superego. Others, such as women with borderline or dependent personalities, will respond with fragility, either having great difficulty managing the anxiety they feel or being unable to hold their own ground in a conflict. These women are often unable to differentiate what is good from what is bad, and cannot set limits or psychic boundaries. Thus, they feel forced to submit to the demands of their partners, becoming compliant or emotionally paralyzed even when their partners' demands are not in their best interests. In essence, the reverse superego's voice says, "Even when I'm good, I will be punished!"

WHY DO WOMEN STAY?

Dutton's (1995) detailed survey leads to the question: "Why do women stay?" "Is there a predisposition for women who stay in abusive attachments?" Loring (1994), Curran (1996), and Lachkar (1997) concur with Dutton (1995) and conclude that there is a predisposition to traumatic bonding. Curran (1996) agrees with most researchers that exposure to parental violence as a child is the strongest predictor of later spousal abuse, and women more often than men are the target of men's aggression. In constructing studies of domination and non-physical abuse, Curran finds that women who have endured verbal, emotional, and psychological abuse, however, have suffered more damage and longer-lasting effects. There is, however, a real division on this point. Some of us—this writer included—believe that even a "healthy" woman can get into the quagmire of abuse, especially when there is intermittent reinforcement. Women *do* have a nesting instinct with specific bonding, emotional attachment, and dependency needs. And therefore, *any* woman can get "caught."

THE ORIGINS OF ABUSE

In understanding that an abused, apparently high-functioning woman lives a conflicted and multi-layered existence, that is, functioning quite successfully in her external working world while experiencing abuse and deprivation in her intimate relationships, the natural question to ask is, how does this dichotomy of achievement and abuse begin and how does it develop? A healthy child, even in infancy, is a resourceful being. Its innate push for development, its capacities to trust, hope, relate, and learn, to be loved and known, all foster growth in this child. When this basic trust is violated, when the natural expectation for love and care is betrayed, the child has no option but to use its innate capacities and strivings to survive, thus trying to preserve who she is. The child cannot leave a depriving or abusive experience—except psychically. In learning to manage its survival, the child returns again and again to try to gain what has been lost, or to achieve what has been withheld by the parent. This early experience sets the stage for the later cycle of enactment of expectation and hope, which then becomes dashed by bitter disappointment in the adult abusive relationship.

Let us now take a brief look at some theorists' ideas to see how they can be applied to the development of this painful cycle and to discover how we can use their ideas to comprehend the ways in which abused, high-functioning women originally struggled with their life experiences.

Freud's instinctual drive theory consisted of two main parts: the Libidinal Drive (part of the Life Instinct or Eros), and the Aggressive Drive (part of the Death Instinct). The Libidinal Drive has a binding capacity, that is, to bring together and hold together. The Death Drive manifests as aggression in its capacity to tear apart, to separate. In a healthy psyche, these drives are always in balance. For instance, in a young child the Libidinal Drive supports the connection to the mother during that phase when such connection is mandatory for the child's growth and maturation. Likewise, the aggressive drive supports the child's emerging ability to become a separate person. However, when the child's earliest strivings are thwarted, the Life Drive becomes her desperate attempt to try to achieve what she needs, with the Death Drive tearing apart the very object that might offer fulfillment of these needs. Internally, the child cannot tolerate its own aggression, and so must repress it, deny it, enact it, or project it. As she grows up, she will either act out this aggression in destructive ways or be drawn to aggression in others, using enormous amounts of energy to keep her internal world separate from the external world in which she lives.

Klein (1957), a follower of Freud, was devoted to Freud's biological psychology. While she agreed with his drive theory, ultimately she came to believe that individuals are more object seeking than drive driven. Klein brought to the forefront the significance of the mother and the breast in mother–infant bonding experiences. She was the first to acknowledge that the early feelings of the child are often experienced as too uncontrollable, terrifying, and volatile to hold inside. When the breast, or the mother, is not providing what the infant needs or wants, the child attempts to rid itself of its feelings by projecting them into the mother. This projective identification serves as the expression of the child's sadistic aggression toward mother's breast and relieves the child of its own internal attacks.

Bion (1977) took Klein's ideas several steps further and developed the notion of normal projective identification, that is, in his container/contained model the mother provides a containing function for the infant's primitive states. In her capacity for reverie, the mother is able to receive the infant's overwhelming and chaotic feelings and to filter them, returning them to the infant in a form that the infant can tolerate and learn to manage. When the mother is unable or unwilling to provide this containing function, the infant is overwhelmed by its own primitive and chaotic affect and is unable to control its terror and rage.

Considering Winnicott's (1965) concept of the true self and false self, let us examine how such an infant must then find some way to protect itself within this state of unbearable affect. When the mother cannot adapt to her infant's needs, and either intrudes her own needs upon the infant or withdraws from the infant, the infant's true self is not fostered. In order to survive this psychic trauma, the infant unconsciously learns to adapt to the mother's needs in order to get its own needs met in some way and to whatever degree possible. To do this, a defensive organization is created—the false self, as Winnicott termed it—to wall off and protect the integrity of the true self. From this early defensive organization, the child continues to adapt to the needs of those around it. However, because the adaptation is made through a continual strengthening of the false self, the individual's actual, true self needs remain unfulfilled. For the high-functioning adult woman, the false self becomes the façade out of which she successfully functions in her external world. But the needs and desires of her true self remain and languish, constantly seeping through. Although the process is an unconscious one, she displaces her legitimate needs and longings onto substitutes: she "needs" to succeed at all costs, she "needs" status and recognition, she "needs" a new diamond bracelet or another trip. The force of her inner yearnings is so powerful, though not understood, that she usually feels entitled to these substitutes. As this woman returns home from the demands and organizing constraints of her professional life, she unconsciously regresses, bringing home as well her powerful and early needs, which appear insatiable—certainly to an abusive partner.

Fairbairn (1940) delineates for us one aspect of why a person stays attached to "bad," rejecting, or unavailable internal objects. Fairbairn maintains that people stay bonded to pain because no matter how excruciating that pain may be, it is still preferable to, and more tolerable than, emptiness. In order to avoid such emptiness, people must remain loyal to their split-off, bad object selves. Grotstein (1990) agrees with this position, offering us the notion that being bonded to pain is better than facing the void, the "black hole." It is the meaningless that evokes states of terror, rather than deprivation or pain.

In applying these theorists' notions, we can begin to see how high-functioning abused women are drawn out of their false self defensive organizations to establishing professional lives of accomplishment and recognition, and how they are also drawn to partners who replicate their original flawed and unfulfilling relationships with their parents. We can also realize how neither their professional lives nor their intimate relationships can provide the fulfillment of the true self needs they are seeking. In their work, they find some validation and satiation of their needs, but in their personal lives, their hopes for connection and fulfillment are thwarted. Their needs for being known and loved for who they are not only remain unmet, but trap them in relationships that diminish them, ultimately leaving them in states of frustration and helplessness.

ABUSE OF HIGH-FUNCTIONING WOMEN

In the endless, unconscious search for the good parent, the good/mommy or good/daddy, the lost object, the mirroring object, the all-encompassing breast, these women seek in intimate partners the idealized object to fill the void. Yet, because of the false-self organization, they never fill the void but instead are faced with painful replications of rejection, withdrawal, or abuse by the original parents. Thus, high-functioning women remain always object seeking but never object finding: "The minute I get home, I feel vilified and belittled. He makes me feel as though I have to always be on the lookout, or else I'm going to get it!" The personal lives of high-functioning, abused women become like a fugue, these themes commingling with the needs and influences of the past, compelling them to continue their search for the caring object, demeaning themselves by acquiescing to the manipulations and control of their partners, and judging themselves as the faulty ones when they meet with rejection, humiliation, or abandonment. The fugue is an apt metaphor, especially as we extend it to encompass the sense of psychic amnesia or unreality these women feel. In this fugue state, various scenarios play out. The women experience fantasies about the abuse in which they grapple with their responsibility for causing it. They suffer an ongoing sense of persecutory anxiety, even in situations where they are competent and not at risk. Or they identify with the abuse: "I must have done something [in reality] to cause the abuse. I deserve the punishment." Such women are not only unable to stand up to the abuse, they are unable to validate their perceptions of it. Often, the issue becomes less the abuse itself than the need for validation that it did or did not occur. "Did it really happen?" becomes a central question, one that remains unanswerable in the absence of anyone serving as an advocate for them. Once a patient feels safe in, and supported by, the therapeutic relationship and environment, exploration of this fugue state is usually where the therapeutic work must begin.

GUIDELINES FOR EMOTIONAL ABUSE

What constitutes emotional abuse? Let us look first at the guidelines (paraphrased) published by Peace at Home, Inc., a human rights organization that addresses not only the severity of domestic violence but calls attention to signs of emotional abuse.

Warning List

Emotional and Economic Attacks

Destructive Criticism/Verbal Abuse: Name-calling, mocking, accusing and/or blaming, yelling, swearing, making humiliating remarks or gestures.

Pressure Tactics: Rushing a partner to make decisions through "guilt-tripping" and other forms of intimidation, sulking, threatening to withhold money, manipulating the children, telling partner what to do.

Abusing Authority: Always claiming to be right (insisting statements are "the truth"), telling partner what to do, making big decisions without consulting partner, using "logic" against partner for one's own gain.

Disrespect: Interrupting, changing topics, not listening or responding, twisting another's words, putting partner down in front of other people, saying bad things about partner's friends and family.

Abusing Trust: Lying, withholding information, cheating on partner, being overly jealous.

Breaking Promises: Not following through on agreements, not taking a fair share of responsibility, refusing to help with child care or housework.

Emotional Withholding: Not expressing feelings, not giving support, attention, or compliments, not respecting feelings, rights or opinions of others.

Minimizing, Denying, and Blaming: Making light of one's own behavior and not taking partner's concerns about it seriously, denying that the abuse happened, shifting responsibility for abusive behavior onto the abused, claiming the abused forced the abuse.

Economic Control: Interfering with partner's work or not letting partner work, refusing to give partner money or taking partner's money, taking partner's car keys or otherwise preventing partner from using the car, threatening to report partner to social service agencies.

Self-Destructive Behavior: Abusing drugs or alcohol, threatening suicide or other forms of self-harm, deliberately saying or doing things that will have negative consequences (e.g., telling off the boss).

Isolation: Preventing or making it difficult for partner to see friends or relatives, monitoring partner's phone calls, telling partner where she can and cannot go.

Harassment: Making uninvited visits or calls, following partner, checking up on her, embarrassing partner in public, refusing to leave when asked.

Intimidation: Making angry or threatening gestures, standing in doorway during arguments, outshouting partner, driving recklessly.

Here we see a wide range of behaviors that many people might justify as possible, even normal, reactions to the stresses of everyday life and intimate relation-ships. Yet, it is essential to understand that the behavior is always at the expense of the other. In no way does it affirm, support, or enhance the other; rather, it demeans, limits, or hurts the other. To the abused, high-functioning woman, this insidious process is not clearly understood. In fact, because these women are high powered and extremely motivated, they have learned to adapt to and absorb the abuse, just as they learned to adapt and absorb it in their early lives. Instead of feeling demeaned by their partners' criticism or disrespect, they have difficulty sleeping or getting up in the morning, feeling the pressure of facing another day. One patient re-marked, "I always feel gloomy and depressed in the morning as though I have nothing to look forward to. But I just get up and manage the day." Rather than feeling the isolation caused by their partners' emotional with-holding, they feel a sense of despair. One patient con-fided, "Sometimes I feel like a robot. I ask myself, 'Is life really worth living?' If it weren't for my work or my children, I wouldn't even want to live. I know I wouldn't do it, but at times I feel like killing myself. Yet, if I told anyone [in my circle] how I feel, no one would believe me. People envy me and can't imagine my pain."

Many victims of emotional abuse report feeling empty and confused. Most feel disconnected: "Unless I'm work-ing I feel like I live in a vacuum. I feel like a nothing." Some report psychosomatic symptoms such as asthma attacks, bronchitis, frequent colds, or back pain. One patient said, "The only time I ever get any attention from my husband is when I'm sick." One woman whose husband was extremely controlling with money, as well as about how she spent her time, commented, "I have such pains and tightness in my chest, I feel as though someone is inside constricting me." She could not see that, in fact, her partner was constricting her; she dealt with his control by converting it into a somatic difficulty, one that would become *her* problem.

In the above examples, we can notice that work—that is, external competence—is the area in which the woman is free of abuse and where she feels the best about herself. Work serves as her refuge. Just as she was originally forced to turn to the outer world for validation and esteem when her internal needs and desires were not met, she returns to it again in order to reinforce that validation. The intrapsychic split between her true self and false self widens even more, as does the split between the rewards of her professional life and the deprivations in her personal one.

CROSS-CULTURAL VIEWS OF WOMEN

A book on emotional abuse cannot exist without some discussion concerning cultural views of gender identity and the role of women. Both of these factors are important in our discussion of the emotional abuse of high-

---

functioning women. Our clinical practices today are filled with couples of various ethnic backgrounds. Cross-cultural, interfaith, and interracial marriages abound. Proponents for the human rights of abused women contend that we need to establish universal guidelines and common ground rules for human rights that take into account the psychohistorical and psychological viewpoints.

Violations of women's rights are part of the broader picture of human rights violations that exists throughout the world. Such groups as Amnesty International, Human Rights Watch, Freedom House, Defense of Human Rights, and Public Liberties advocate strict guidelines in holding human rights violators accountable. America will soon be targeting groups and nations that disenfranchise women. So strong is this growing pressure that many Americans will deny support to foreign governments that tolerate or promote discrimination against women. Increasing consciousness and commitment to women's rights will be redefined to make equal treatment of women abroad a top priority.

As an example of such violations, it has been noted that in some Arab countries as well as in other parts of the world, clitoridectomy, or female circumcision, is still practiced. Circumcision is most often performed on female children at the age of seven or eight (before the girl begins to get her period). Describing the practice, Patai (1983) notes that on the day of the circumcision, midwives and female family members grasp the child's thighs on either side, then pull them apart to expose the external organs. A sharp razor is used to cut off the clitoris. Clitoridectomy, like all genital mutilations, is a harsh and perverse act (deMause 1991); it represents the acting out of frustration and aggression on innocent victims. Genital mutilation has nothing to do with "rites of passage." In fact, it is the gateway to trauma and destruction for any child and any society.

For women, circumcision is designed to curtail their sexuality and to keep their desires repressed. Girls not only go through excruciating pain, but they faint from shock (no anesthetic); suffer tetanus, blood poisoning, chronic urinary tract infections, and infertility; have severe complications at childbirth, and unbearable pain during intercourse; and sometimes die, usually from hemorrhage. Some of these women have come into treatment in the United States, recounting these horror stories. Today women's groups are demanding action. The following is from the *Human Rights Watch Global Report on Women's Human Rights* (1997):

> Women are murdered beaten, raped, traded as chattel, denied their independence, and marginalized in many ways—often with the active participation or deliberate indifference of government officials. This state of neglect has dramatically changed over the last two decades as women's groups mobilized to challenge gender-related

abuse. Increasingly, they are also collaborating with human rights organizations. Working together, these two movements are exchanging information and developing strategies for protecting and promoting women's rights that are not only morally persuasive, but also legally enforceable. [p. 1]

Women in the United States from other cultures sometimes have very different perceptions as to what constitutes abuse. In Saudi Arabia, Muslim women view American women as abused and sexually exploited because they must live in isolation without extended families to provide a community, must work while raising a family, and must live in a society increasingly dominated by drugs, divorce, and violence. Conversely, American women view these Muslim women as abused because they must be submissive to men, and are seen as men's possessions or chattel. Further, the American woman will be hard pressed to understand a Saudi Arabian woman who, for a variety of reasons, has a child forcibly taken away from her. In the United States, the American woman has the opportunity to fight to her last breath for her child; yet, in Saudi Arabia the woman will deal with her loss by using her group as a "container" to hold her pain. Subject to systematic discrimination by cultural customs that relegate her to an inferior and unequal status, she will accept her fate.

How do these conflicting cultural views of women

and their rights—or absence of them—apply to the topic of emotional abuse of high-functioning women? Today's influx of immigrants from around the world, with the resultant clash of cultural values, has become the norm in many places in the United States. Our clinical practices are filled with couples from various ethnic backgrounds.

Let us look at two examples of cross-cultural couples. In the first example, a clinician is treating a Japanese wife and an American husband. The husband is proud of his professional wife, a designer, yet he also enjoys her doting on him, and her many ways of making their home a sanctuary. The conflicts in the marriage emerged after the couple's first child began to grow out of infancy.

The husband, an attorney, felt suffocated by his wife's tendency to infantilize their son. Even though the child was over a year old, the husband did not understand, nor was he comfortable with, his wife's doting on the child. "I can't stand it, she's arranged to take our son to work with her, and all she does is hold him and breast-feed him, and she doesn't let him cry. She attends to his every whim. This just isn't right. She says she wants peace and harmony for the boy and doesn't want him to grow up like these 'ambitious' Americans."

It is interesting to note that as long as the wife's doting was geared toward the husband, all was well. What the American husband did not understand was that the doting mother's preoccupation with her male son was appropriate in Japanese child-rearing practices. Japanese mothers are extremely empathic, and even indulgent by Western standards. There is a special Japanese word, *amae*, to describe this mother–child relationship. It is a form of dependency understood as the mother's intense internalization and identification with her child's, and especially her male child's, needs. Put another way, *amae* is a dependency need that manifests itself in a longing to merge with others. The eminent Japanese psychoanalyst Takeo Doi (Doi 1973, Johnson 1994) called *amae* a key concept for understanding Japanese personality structure. The concept of *amae* is very complex, and has been the subject of debate among Japanese and American analysts. But back to the American husband who was competing with her son for the doting mother's breast. This conflict in the relationship was heavily steeped in cross-cultural differences, and that is where the marriage ran into difficulty.

In our second example, we note the pressures emerging in a marriage of some ten years between an American wife, a real estate broker, and her Muslim husband, a real estate investor. Originally, their marriage went smoothly because of mutual goals and interests. With the arrival of two children, and traveling to the Middle East for family visits, the marriage began to erode.

Abdul: I really don't want to be here, because I don't believe in therapy. In my country this is unheard of. If we have a problem, we pray to Allah for forgiveness, and our will and destiny are in His hands.

Mary: This is what my children and I have to put up with all the time. I don't believe in prayer, magical thinking, wishes, dreams. I am a practical person, well educated and well informed, and can't believe I'm with someone who does all this "hokey-pokey stuff." I believe in talking things over and working things out. Everytime there's a problem, Abdul talks about Allah. Can't he realize he's in America now? This is not the Middle East. When there were just the two of us, I could ignore it, but now, this is very difficult for our children.

Therapist: Yes, it does sound as though there are some real cultural differences that are causing stress and very hurtful feelings.

Mary: We went to Saudi Arabia last year and took the children to visit Abdul's parents. My daughters and I vowed we would not wear our veils [chadors], but when we arrived there we were wearing our American garb and we found ourselves being stared down. Not only were we viewed as foreign and strange, their eyes were burning through our clothes. On the street, the men were looking at us as if we were prostitutes.

Abdul: (laughing) Yes, and you should have seen how quick they put on their chadors and hijabs. Have you

ever visited my country? There, the women don't
even have a say. They aren't even allowed an opinion. My wife doesn't know how lucky she is that I am
not like that.

Mary: He may not be like that, but he doesn't realize how
difficult it has become to talk freely. Maybe we can do
that here.

While these two examples do not show couples
involved in severe enactments of abuse, each couple has
experienced the shift from a harmonious relationship in
which their cultural differences were at least benign if not
appreciated, to a relationship where the cultural differences are beginning to threaten the marriage. Without
resolution, the shift could become more profound, bringing with it increased alienation and, ultimately, emotional abuse.

It is difficult for therapists to find their way through
the thicket of cultural issues. And it is an additional
burden for therapists to familiarize themselves with
issues surrounding human rights, to find special modali-
ties to meet the treatment needs of these women. Finding
some universal guidelines that take into account instinctual drives, basic infant bonding stages of development,
and the resolution of the Oedipus complex is of paramount importance. Some critics of human rights prefer to
attribute what I call abuse to cultural relativism, arguing
that there are traditions, laws, and ideologies that justify

the aggression (rooted in culture and religion). Endleman (1989) disputes this argument. He distinguishes the transcultural from the more commonly used term, "crosscultural." The term "transcultural" applies to basic psychic universalities, for instance, basic issues around human development, and the employment of mechanisms of defense (repression, denial, splitting, projection, projective identification). I am in agreement with Endleman's point of view. And thus, I feel that while cultural traditions are not to be neglected, aggression and mistreatment of women (reflected in our clinical practices) cannot be condoned.

Gender Identification

In the examination of the emotional abuse of high-functioning women, our discussion must include the issue of gender and the contrariety of identification. Gender identification deals with the establishment of who we are, our basic sense of being male or female, our identification with the parent of the same gender or of the opposite gender. In healthy development, the formation of our gender identity is a normal process, the achievement of which serves as a developmental marker. Gender identity formation relates to the primary identification with the mother (Chasseguet-Smirgel 1970, Stoller 1975), is considered a component of the separation-individuation phase of psychological development, and is thought to be consolidated by the successful attainment of object constancy. The establishment of our identity as female or male has three aspects: (1) our internalization of the actual distinction between female and male, (2) our identification with those of our own gender, and (3) the recognition that the two genders both have their own functions, which exist in complementary juxtaposition with each other, especially in the area of reproduction.

Sexual identity is not the same thing as gender identity but is part of a later stage of the development of gender identification. Similarly, gender identity is not synonymous with either gender role or behavior. These aspects of gender identity are determined culturally, forming behavior patterns that the culture considers appropriate and desirable for males and females. It is in this arena that our cultural stereotypes exert great influence. Today, we no longer make traditional assignments of sex roles and psychological gender characteristics. Instead, we are aware that the development of characteristics that are considered part of maleness or femaleness is a complex process.

This awareness can help us comprehend some of the influences on women and men that impel them to conform to, or rebel against, certain stereotypes of femaleness or maleness. Many high-functioning women have disidentified with their mothers, who represent the feminine, and have taken on the attributes of their fathers, who represent the masculine. These women usually defend against their dependency needs, fearing them to be dangerous and psychically threatening. Yet, rejection of these needs does not mean that they disappear, and so we find that these high-functioning women must repeatedly grapple with the pain found in living a split life—a successful professional life juxtaposed against an unfulfilling personal life. What gets lost in this split is the possibility of actually having one's true needs met or of ever living a mutually respectful, mutually loving life with a partner.

Feminism

Originally feminism was a doctrine advocating social and political rights for women equal to those of men, and it became an organized movement for the attainment of such reforms for women. Under the umbrella of altruism and willingness to do good, the movement gradually became infested with signs of mania and aggression. Even a "good" cause can be a violation. Just as a spouse or parent can emotionally abuse us, so can a cause, a movement, or an organization.

As with many organized movements, factions began to develop and feminism began to be applied to issues other than equal rights and equal pay, issues concerning gender identity, dependence versus independence, cooperation versus aggression. Issues of equality became confused at times with issues of sameness, where the differences in feminine and masculine identity were no longer appreciated or validated, and thus they were considered by some to be specious. Women's dependency needs became a sign of weakness, their aggression and independence a sign of strength. Unfortunately, for many women, this invalidation of their dependency needs served only to replicate the early denial of such needs by their parents.

Contemporary feminism has begun to recognize women as multifaceted and as having distinct characteristics, values, and roles that are equal to, but not the same as, those of men. The positive forces in feminism are striving to help women learn to live a life of mutuality and interdependence. Women are viewed as separate persons who also must function as the primary caregivers in their capacities as mothers. While Benjamin (1988) argues that no psychological theory has adequately articulated the mother's independent existence, she clearly states the importance of mutual recognition— mother as part of the baby's object needs and mother as her own independent subject.

Although today's woman would not dream of giving up her independence, many women throughout the world who have had a taste of emancipation are taking a second look at the exhortations of hard-line feminism. After years of being Superwoman, maintaining two jobs, cooking, shopping, taking care of children, working during the day only to come home to more work (even if they have husbands who participate in caregiving and household duties), nowadays many are craving the more traditional role. In being exposed to the joys and satisfactions of an independent life, women were not cautioned as to the price such a life could exact. Further, for women who live out of their false-self organizations within abusive relationships, such demands only exacerbate the pressures and requirements of their original life experiences. More than ever, it is essential that women have a supportive and non-threatening counterpart. The challenge in learning to function as an autonomous, self-actualized, and successful woman is also to learn how to re-establish one's true self and be drawn to those intimate relationships that can nurture true self needs and in which one can live a life of mutuality.

✌❧ 2 ☙✌

Love Bonds

After years of effort, Michelle now holds the position of city planner for a mid-sized city. She is dedicated to the community's needs and is a strong and empathic leader of the team she heads. Knowledgeable in the area of finance, she has been ingenious in finding ways to establish the sense of old-fashioned values and surroundings in an upscale city, satisfying the needs of its inhabitants for a safe and charm-filled place to live. When her day finishes, she looks once again to her relationship of five years to fulfill the same needs she carries internally and that she meets for others: emotional safety, charm, warmth, and space in which to grow. What she finds instead is a partner who measures out his affection in spoonfuls, according to his taste. Within moments of coming home, she feels herself consumed by anxiety about how to make him happy. She knows, too, as she heads for the kitchen and another meal preparation, that she will both fail and stay. And she wonders why.

In considering emotional abuse, we ask ourselves what it is that draws and keeps these partners together. As we have seen in the previous chapter, at the heart of these painful and destructive relationships exist many unfulfilled archaic wishes, longings, and fantasies. Individuals with split-off or repressed needs, or those whose needs have been thwarted or denied, become magnets, drawing to themselves various kinds of abusive partners.

With this in mind, we then ask ourselves what the typology is of women who stay with abusive men. In my clinical practice, I was treating a patient population comprised increasingly of women who were well educated, high functioning, and successful in their professional careers, but who were also emotionally abused in their most intimate relationships. I found myself wondering how women who appear so intelligent and accomplished can resort to such primitive behaviors in their personal relationships. Further, I wondered whether there were universal or typical patterns fueling the interactions between abusive men and high-functioning women. These questions and the answers I found prompted me to write this book.

Despite patients' individual histories and unique personalities, I noted certain common themes in these abusive relationships. Kernberg's (1990) work on romantic love and the polymorphous fusion of the couple helps us comprehend how sadomasochism, perversion, hate, envy, and erotic desire are connected with libidinal aspects of early object relations and primitive defenses. Kernberg's ideas are unique because they recognize the complexities of the love relationship and the "private madness" of the couple.

WHY DO PEOPLE STAY
IN PAINFUL RELATIONSHIPS?

In describing sadomasochistic relations, Kernberg (1992) provides valuable material that helps us understand, in particular, the emotional abuse of women. One of his key points is that men tend to be more aggressive than women, and are inclined to form sadistic attachments. Kernberg's work on romantic love and the polymorphous fusion of the couple illuminates how a preponderance of envy, greed, domination, and control overpowers the capacity for intimacy and love. Kernberg (1990, 1991a,b) masterfully describes how the interplay between love and aggression can determine the capacity for intimacy and how sexual excitement incorporates aggression. Aggression, according to Kernberg, can be employed in two ways: in the service of love or as a retreat from love. In pathological or abusive bonds, internal strivings for control and domination interfere with the capacity to maintain an intimate attachment. In more perverse relations sexual excitement can be used as a replacement for love.

In *Aggression in Personality Disorders and Perversions* Kernberg (1992) describes four kinds of love relationships: (1) normal love, (2) pathological love, (3) perverse love, and (4) mature love. His premise is that in normal love, the relationship overcomes the conflict. Internal strivings do not interfere with the individual's capacity to maintain an intimate, passionate, love relationship. But in pathological love, conflict overpowers the relationship. Internal conflicts interfere with the relationship, reducing love to states of distress. In normal relations, individuals are effectively reassured by reality testing. These are the kinds of couples who benefit from short-term psychotherapy. However, in pathological bonds reality testing does not offer relief; instead, it is replaced by infantile functioning, and primarily the loss of self (Vaquer 1991). These couples are in need of more intensive psychotherapy (individual therapy in addition to conjoint sessions). In short, Kernberg's key point is that aggression may be used either in promoting love or in moving away from love. When aggressive energy, which is inherent in everyone, is not utilized in constructive, adaptive, egosyntonic ways, its fury and power erupt in destructive ways.

Kernberg's understanding of aggression provided a valuable touchstone for me as I turned my attention to the emotional abuse of high-functioning women. I began to consider more deeply how aggression can be used in the service of love. In healthy adult relationships, even though there may be conflict and aggression, the partners are able to live in mutuality and interdependence. They are nurtured by their commonality as well as by their differences, fostering one another's growth by moving within the ebb and flow of their own autonomous strivings while also meeting the needs of the other. The conflicts that emerge within the interactions of two dynamic people do not interfere with their capacity to maintain a loving and intimate relationship. When conflict does occur, the nature of the relationship supports the resolution of the conflict and the partners are able to talk and work together to find respectful and mutually beneficial solutions. At the core of such relationships is the desire for unification, harmony, and synchronicity. In abusive relationships, desire is sabotaged by internal forces. As conflicts overcome the relationship, they become the focus of much of its emotional energy. Anger festers and explodes, and abandonment fears soar. Domination, control, submission, and envy create a continual competitive match. Conflicts turn into power struggles, pitting one partner against the other. Feelings and needs are unwelcome strangers or dangerous interlopers. Words are not used for communication, but for distraction and avoidance.

In an abusive relationship, professional careers, goals, or ambitions can be a severe threat to the relationship. Healthy dependency needs, or any tentative movement toward growth, development, or separation-individuation are experienced as dangerous saboteurs. Thus, ambivalence in success is fostered; the reaching for status and wealth is accompanied by the negative implication that the success was neither earned nor deserved.

In healthy relationships, there must be a basic desire to please and nourish the other. This desire is the willingness to honor the needs and hopes of the other. Such willingness does not preclude the responsibility of each partner to honor and attend to his or her own needs, but it does mean that there is a concern for the other's general sense of well-being. We find in mature love the natural extension of normal love. In mature love, each partner gives priority to the other for the common good. The couple forms a unit, and while remaining two separate individuals, they function inter- dependently, their aims and dreams working in harmony. As mature love grows, there is a deepening of the relationship. In the early stages of romantic love, love is for the sake of love; the two partners are momentarily "insane." Romantic love knows no bounds and conquers all. Passion carries more importance than the emotional needs of the other. In mature love, this "insanity" is tempered by a growing knowledge of the other and the desire to be in mutuality; earlier passionate sexuality becomes infused with a shared intimacy. The partnership endures the stresses and strains of ever-changing roles and the partners are able to accept the responsibility both for recognizing the realities of life and also continu- ing to nourish one another's goals.

Kernberg's (1991a,b) elaborations point to what hap- pens in couples' intimate relations when a preponder- ance of envy, greed, and control overpowers the capacity for intimacy and love. In normal relationships, love and passion are linked to healthy eroticism, with the couple's inherent aggression used to nurture and maintain intimacy. In pathological love, aggression is used to destroy intimacy. Love and passion in the erotic life of such couples are experienced as power plays, with excitement created at the expense of the other. Sadomasochistic enactments become the vehicles for expressing aggression in the perpetrator and vengeful feelings in the victim.

In perverse love, there exists a basic confusion over what is good and what is bad. What is good is considered bad; what is bad is converted into good. In such a relationship, normal love cannot thrive. Perversity does not refer only to whips and chains but to the entire spectrum that it can cover, from severe acts of cruelty to the seemingly benign. In one relationship, a husband withholds sex when his wife does not prepare the dinner he desired, then attacks her for being an unsuitable sexual partner. In another, a woman is rebuffed every time she tries to hold her husband's hand; he says she is too clingy. In these instances, physical contact is transformed into a negative act instead of an essential ingredient of an intimate relationship.

In Kernberg's view, perverse love often becomes the replacement for normal or mature love, because perverse love is the individual's emotional insurance against the liability of getting too close to the "good thing." Perversion serves as the antithesis to intimacy; erotic stimulation substitutes for love. The sexual act that emanates from perverse love becomes an avoidance of intimacy and bonding, and instead interfaces with cruelty, sadism, and hatred.

Perversions may be distinguished not only by perverse acts in and of themselves but by the level at which the acts are organized. Bach (1994) notes that distinctions between normality and perversion lie within the realm of experience. Bach, as well as Kernberg, has broadened the conceptualization of perversions to encompass not only sexual encounters but character disorders. As Bach states, from a "certain perspective one might say that a person has a perversion instead of having a relationship" (p. 3).

Kernberg maintains that men are constitutionally more aggressive and thus more sadistic than women, while women are more masochistic than men. Why might this be so? I believe that in our culture, young boys are taught that their neediness is unmasculine. Boys are encouraged to disidentify from the mother, the feminine, in order to become men, and so many of their dependency needs must be repressed, split off, and/or projected. Young girls face a different problem. Though permitted to be more dependent or "needy," they find as they grow up they are expected to repress their needs in order to concentrate on the benevolent task of fulfilling the needs of others. In short, they are taught to identify with their mothers, often in the role of the caregiver. While aggression is touted as a positive trait in boys, girls must learn to express their aggression, emotional and sexual, in more covert ways. Thus, the stage is set for men and women to come together prepared not for intimate attachments and mutuality, but rather for the psychic battleground of manipulating and controlling one another as they attempt to get their disowned or disguised needs met.

THE DANCE BETWEEN THE ABUSER
AND THE ABUSED

The metaphor of the dance offers us a provocative image with which to understand the compelling draw and interactions between partners in emotionally abusive relationships. In this dance, unconscious fantasies are enacted and reenacted, some dances sinuous, some fervent, some erotic, some raging. The different aspects of the dance are composed of the interlocking behaviors of the partners, each eliciting profound vulnerabilities and unresolved conflicts in the other. This dance portrays a cruel and paradoxical fact: the partner who is loved and adored is also the partner who is felt to be the bitter enemy. The partner who is abusive is also the same one who promises hope and intimacy. It is the loved and hated parent.

Projective identification is a term devised by Klein (1952) and expanded by, among others, Bion (1968) and Grotstein (1981). I believe it is useful in understanding the dance of the couple. I envision the dance as involving "dual projective identifications" (Lachkar 1992), in which both partners project unwanted parts of themselves into one another. Projective identification is a one-way process whereby one person projects a "bad" feeling into the object, usually a part of the self felt to be intolerable. Dual projective identification is a two-way process whereby both partners are vigorously engaged in projecting back and forth, internalizing and identifying with the other's projections. The metaphor of the dance helps us understand that both the abuser and the abused share an emotional investment in the enactments that generate abuse.

Many high-functioning women learned long ago to split off the needs they considered unacceptable. When such a woman forms an intimate relationship, she projects these early split-off or repressed yearnings and needs into her partner. While the partner identifies with the projection, he cannot tolerate the dependency that such an identification produces. In order to get rid of these evoked needs he then abuses the woman, lashing out against the identification he has assumed, that is, his sense of dependency. In turn, when the woman is abused, the violation punishes her for her original and projected needs, and serves to assuage her guilt.

Or, let us look at another version of the dance. A high-functioning woman uses her aggression to productive ends in her workplace environment. Yet, when she returns home, she looks to her partner for caregiving and tenderness. When this emotional hunger is not met, she becomes wounded, possibly angry. Her aggression, which is acceptable and perhaps even admirable at work, now becomes unacceptable rage, and so once again she is in a double bind. Unconsciously, the partner accepts the projection and acts out the rage against the woman. This enactment confirms her innate sense of hopelessness: she can now blame her partner as the cause of her despair.

What draws two partners together in the dance of emotional abuse is the nature of the relationship between their bad internal objects and the bad external objects they choose. As we examine different types of emotionally abusive "dances," it is essential to keep in mind the dialectic relationship men and women establish as they play out and experience each other's internal and external objects. Both men and women unconsciously gravitate to the object choices best patterned to meet some unfulfilled or split-off part of the self.

THE NON-ENTITLED SELF/THE DEPRIVING OBJECT

Rebecca's early life was marked by severe deprivation. Her mother performed the perfunctory obligations of parenting: feeding her, bathing her, and clothing her, but there was little physical holding or cuddling. Her father, a salesman, traveled sometimes weeks on end. When he returned home, his needs predominated; he needed time and caretaking to nurse the wounds from the rejection he often experienced on the road. While the household was never consumed by financial poverty, there was an emotional poverty that lay like a shroud over every member of the family. When Rebecca grew up, she paid her way through college and graduate school, becoming a professor of English literature. She was drawn to a man who seemed charismatic and who was extremely successful as a computer salesman. Rebecca, as a practiced caregiver, saw to his every need, never asking anything for herself. Her non-entitled self did not believe she deserved anything from this man. As the unavailable object, he unconsciously agreed. In twenty years of marriage, he never bought her a birthday or anniversary gift.

THE LOST SELF/THE IDEALIZED OBJECT

Philip inherited a fortune from his entrepreneurial father. Living in the shadow of this dynamic man, Philip became a biochemical researcher, but was unable to take many risks in life. He married Victoria, a hospital administrator who was especially adept at collecting large sums of money from wealthy contributors to the hospital. Victoria seemingly had it all: she was stunning to look at, bright, and vivacious. Philip's self-effacing nature provided the perfect counterpart to her effervescent personality. He idealized and adored her, the light she exuded warming his shadowed self. But over time, Victoria felt ashamed of Philip's wimpishness. His adoration sickened her. She railed against his emotional impotence, which soon found expression in his sexual impotence. He retaliated by needling her, converting the very aspects he had previously adored into objects of ridicule and belittlement. She withdrew. He felt abandoned and lost all over again. He rediscovered her, idealized her, pursued her: their dance continued.

THE CRAVING SELF/THE UNAVAILABLE OBJECT

Carol was highly excited by Vivian, whom she regarded as warm and nurturing. Carol craved Vivian's love, even more so when Vivian showed interest in others. Carol confided: "Vivian gives people so much attention; this is why I fell in love with her. She seemed so caring of everyone."

In the beginning, Vivian showered Carol with affection and praise. Carol, an emotionally starved young woman hidden in a high-functioning false self, could not get enough of Vivian's attentions. Craving unconditional and limitless expressions of love, Carol became possessive, wanting Vivian to turn away from her involvements with others. She said, "Vivian goes off nearly every weekend now to be with friends, only to return with endless stories of her encounters. I cringe with envy, becoming enraged as I listen to her tales of compassion for others."

Vivian complained that she could not tolerate Carol's demands: "I just want to run away from Carol when she becomes so possessive. She is very aggressive towards me. This is not the woman I fell in love with."

Both Carol and Vivian felt victimized by one another. Vivian experienced Carol as a replication of her intruding and violating mother; Carol was terrified by Vivian's unavailability and responded to it by increasing her demands.

THE WRONGED SELF/THE REJECTING OBJECT

Lanelle was raised by a brilliant but alcoholic attorney father and a terrified artistic mother. Domination and submission were the themes of her parents' lives. As her father's legal career plummeted from a partnership in a prestigious law firm to an ever-shrinking private practice of ambulance-chasing cases, his sadism and aggressive control dominated the household. As she grew older, Lanelle's attempts at preventing her father's physical abuse of her mother resulted in her father's unleashing verbal storms of abuse at her. During sober times, his warmth and interest and promises to reform were seductive.

Lanelle became a public defense attorney. She chose as her husband a painter and sculptor, an introspective man who apparently desired the kind of peaceful life she did. In the early stages of their relationship, both partners seemed to flourish. Lanelle did not mind being the primary financial support of the family; she believed in her husband's talent. Stewart appreciated the opportunity to devote himself to the development of his work, and rewarded his wife with gourmet dinners accompanied by classical music and candlelight. They agreed never to have children.

When Lanelle unexpectedly became pregnant and could not bear to have an abortion, the marriage began to unravel. Since she was unable to reduce her work load because she was on the "partner track," the care of their infant son fell to her husband. In the first months of the baby's life, Stewart was able to combine his creative work with parenting. But as the baby reached toddlerhood, Stewart's work in his home studio suffered. Soon, he began to blame Lanelle for her insistence on having the child and the burdens and changes this had imposed on their lives. A move to a new studio away from the house and the hiring of a nanny did not change Stewart's attacks against Lanelle or his rejection of her and their son. Lanelle was caught again in the intervening position she had learned in childhood, interventions that cost her dearly.

THE DIFFERENT KINDS
OF ABUSERS AND ABUSED

The above stories are typical of the cases that find their way to my consulting room. Each demonstrates a different form of the dance between the abuser and the abused. Each exemplifies the entrapment involved in dual projective identification. I will now outline four themes that repeat in almost every abusive relationship:

1. In the dual projective identification process, the partners in the relationship recreate the behaviors they experienced at the hands of their neglectful, depriving, or abusive parents, parents who at times also behaved in loving ways.

2. Between the partners in an abusive relationship, there is often a lack of awareness of or an indifference to the suffering of the other, and a preoccupation with the suffering of oneself. Further, there is an inability to decipher what is cruel and what is not. The validation of cruelty, not only cruelty expressed by the other, but also expressed by oneself, is one of the first steps toward answering the often asked question: "Is this really happening? Or am I crazy?"

3. Within each partner there is an intolerance of being criticized, an unrealistic view of dependency needs, and an inability to cope with frustration.

These difficulties are dealt with by the use of control, withdrawal, non-validation, and attack.
4. Each partner experiences entitlement and deprivation. When such entitlement is present there is not a big enough house, a car with enough status, enough trips, a prestigious enough school for one's children, or even a good enough table at the most upscale restaurant. When a material need is satisfied, the satisfaction is momentary, soon replaced by a deeper, more desperate sense of deprivation.

Initially, when partners in an intimate relationship seek treatment, it is common for them to think they are talking about the relationship when they focus on who pays the mortgage, who does the disciplining of the children, who controls the money, who demands the most sex, who is tight with time, or who went out of the way to make the other jealous. While they are partially right—any of these enactments is reflective of the problems in the relationship—they also are indirect ways of talking about internal difficulties with dependency needs, boundaries, the management of frustration, and separation anxiety. In the early stages of therapy, the relationship can serve as the transitional object to each partner's internal world.

Just as there are many different types of character disorders, there are many different types of abusers and those who are abused. By diagnosing and learning how to treat the qualitative differences among the various kinds of abusers and abused, we become more finely attuned not only to the perpetrators' typologies, but to the kinds of women who stay with them and their motivations for doing so. Within that framework we can then consider the reality of the abuse and the unconscious fantasies concerning the abuse, so that finally we can begin to alter the dynamics within each partner and thereby the dynamics of the relationship as well. In those cases where such alterations are not possible, the therapist needs to help the partners to let go of the relationship.

What follows in the next five chapters are my own classifications of different emotional abusers, abstracted from current diagnostic personality categories. Within each chapter, as I focus on the narcissistic abuser, the borderline abuser, the passive-aggressive abuser, the obsessive-compulsive abuser, and the schizoid abuser, there is: (1) a description of the abuser's disorder, including his archaic, unresolved conflicts and defenses, and the enactments he employs; (2) a typology of the high-functioning women who are drawn to and stay with these men; (3) case illustrations, which demonstrate how the dance is enacted according to the couple's strivings for intimate attachments; and, last, (4) some preliminary treatment suggestions.

ᯇ 3 ᯇ

The Narcissistic Abuser

I try to hold his hand; I try to get him to notice me. Even when I'm all dressed up, he acts as if I were nothing! Nothing excites him. The only time he pays any attention to me is when we speak about money, futures, stocks, bonds, or anything else that will empower him.

THE NARCISSIST

In his initial formulations about narcissism, Freud (1914) refers to it as the state of self-directed libido, just as in the Greek legend of Narcissus who fell in love with his own image. In trying to tackle the complexity of narcissism, Freud refers to "his majesty the baby," and how his omnipotent self impacts the narcissist's ability to fall in love. Originally, Freud conceived of primary narcissism as occurring when the self is taken as the love object. Later, he replaced this notion with that of secondary narcissism, which covers a spectrum from normal to pathological narcissism. Due to disappointments, the self withdraws its libidinal investment in the external object and reinvests the self, or, in common parlance, one stops loving the other and loves oneself. In excess—as with Narcissus—the individual appears to love himself or herself too much.

The Kohutian (1971, 1977) model of narcissism depicts a more highly developed narcissistic individual whose primary and normal narcissistic needs were inadequately met at phase-appropriate times (Lachkar 1992). The developmental arrest in the child's archaic grandiose self and in his idealized parental representations infringes on the completion of a cohesive self. Thus the child becomes an adult who is vulnerable to "fragmentation" and "depletion" whenever disappointment or frustration occurs.

Willi (1962) describes collusive patterns of interactions of couples as derived from unresolved oedipal conflict. He saw love as "oneness in narcissistic collusion" and was on the right track when he discovered particular kinds of couples forming narcissistic bonds similar to the patterns outlined here. The narcissist longs for unattainable perfection in both self and other. The most dominant features of the narcissistic personality disorder are the pervasive patterns of grandiosity and omnipotence, a constant need for approval and admiration, a general lack of concern and empathy for others, and a pronounced sense of entitlement. The emotional life of narcissistic personalities is shallow, as they receive very little satisfaction from life other than from the adulation they receive from others. Narcissists confuse normal states of vulnerability with imperfection. When not responded to or "properly" mirrored, narcissistic personalities will either physically or emotionally withdraw. In more severe cases, narcissists are unable to recognize needs, and are quick to obliterate or diminish the needs of others.

By the very nature of their personality structures, most narcissists create pain in their love objects (usually borderline or dependent types). This occurs because the developmentally arrested narcissist has a false self, that is, a grandiose non-needy self. His true self needs are intolerable, and thus he projects these needs into his borderline partner, whom he then diminishes and rejects, and from whom he ultimately withdraws.

THE NARCISSISTIC ABUSER

The emotionally abusive narcissist is the "entitlement lover," in love only with self, unable to imagine that the needs of others exist. If he does imagine such needs, he cannot conceive that they might differ from his own. He has unreasonable expectations of others, and will often take advantage of them. Because of the inability to feel or show dependency needs, he exacerbates feelings of inadequacy and shame in the love object. Often these men choose very needy, clingy, or possessive women who will stir up their own split-off needy side. The narcissist will complain: "If only she would give me my space and not make any demands upon me, then I could be more available to her."

The narcissist cannot allow himself the kind of dependency an intimate partner yearns for because the exposure would make him feel too vulnerable and threaten him with fragmentation. Obsessed with perfectionism, narcissists must continually prove their sense of specialness. Frequently, they have internalized a punitive superego, one that makes them unduly critical of self and object. When their sense of pride is threatened they will withdraw either physically or emotionally, or respond with narcissistic rage: "I don't need you, I don't need this treatment, and I don't need this relationship!" In their proclamations of self-perfection, they may form sadomasochistic ties or may be experienced by their partners as sadistic. Since the narcissists' libidinal love ties are directed toward themselves and away from caring or concern for others, communication becomes virtually impossible.

One can imagine how a malignant narcissist with masochistic pathology affects the abused woman, especially a high-functioning woman who may combine with her external competence an inner sense of fragility. In emotionally abusive ties, the narcissist's superego demands are such that they create states of paralysis in the object, especially if one is so inclined to identify with them. One patient who became overwhelmed by her narcissistic partner's rage and put-downs remarked recently: "Why do I get so frozen? Why can't I just open up a book and read? I just sit there and stare. I had a dream about monsters and bears. When I was little, I was afraid to move for fear the bears would get me, and to this day, when he does this I become paralyzed."

THE NARCISSISTS' DEFENSES

Narcissists are dominated by such defenses as idealization, omnipotence, and grandiosity. Many narcissists were once their mother's only and/or favorite child until their crown was usurped by a new sibling. The birth of a younger brother or sister is often a traumatic event for a child, evoking feelings of being replaced, substituted for, and neglected. One patient revealed an account of what was for him a harrowing experience. When he was a five-year-old child, his mother went away for a few days without saying good-bye or explaining where she was going. Each day he remained glued to the window, gripping the curtains, waiting for a glimpse of his mother. When he finally saw her she had a "package" in her arms; it was his new baby sister.

Narcissists who live in narcissistic nostalgia may spend their lives trying to recapture the earlier position of specialness. A child who is left emotionally hungry by an unempathic mother or a mother who is dominant, intrusive, or cold will have great difficulty overcoming rivalry or resolving oedipal issues. In the relationship arena, these men often engage in endless competitive matches. Often unable to forgive the parents for the upheaval of being replaced, the child may grow up perceiving the parents as cruel, rejecting, or sadistic, and take refuge in a part of himself that is designed to get even. "I'll show them! I'll become famous, and they'll be sorry!" As these needs and affects become too powerful to contain, they invariably get projected (often into someone with a vulnerable character structure, who already has a thwarted sense of self and who then feels diminished, and ultimately abandoned).

A couple in their mid-fifties, each with grown children from first marriages, are having dinner with the wife's adult children. The husband accuses the wife: "Susan, you gave everyone at the dinner table something to eat first, and you totally ignored me. You gave your son a chicken breast, and what did you give me? You gave me the backs!"

In this scenario, the borderline wife has unconsciously projected into her narcissistic husband that he is not entitled to "the breast," an enactment playing into his original narcissistic injury that he was not entitled to his mother's breast after his baby brother was born.

THE HIGH-FUNCTIONING PARTNER
OF THE NARCISSISTIC ABUSER

The type of woman the narcissistic abuser most often attracts is the borderline. While these women may be high functioning professionally and in many of their interpersonal relations, the borderline aspects of their personalities take hold when they become involved in intimate relationships. This dichotomy has usually been present since childhood. The original damage they experienced occurred through the unavailability of, or lack of attunement from, the parents. These women often had to sacrifice their childhood needs in order to take on the role of caring for others; they had to be the responsible ones, the caretakers of younger siblings or their own parents. Some may have had to act as mediators or even therapists as they were drawn into parental battles. They grew up emotionally starved, being taught that their own dependency needs were bad and dangerous, and they learned to take any crumbs offered to them.

As they were growing up, these young children had to learn to deal with the fallout from such deprivation, that is, their emerging rage, hatred, and jealousy, and their own sadistic urges. Using the defenses of reaction formation, repression, or splitting, they overcompensated for their overwhelming affect by becoming overly caring and exceedingly kind. As adults, many of these border-line women suffer from severe depression relating to the conflicts from their early childhood or adolescence. Never learning how to mourn, or how to deal with sadness, loss, or depression, they develop addictive personalities, often expressed through eating disorders. They may pursue affairs in their desperate search for love, and in the most intense enactment of the search, they find ways of parasitically attaching to their objects. A typical example is a string of endless suicide threats as a way to try to keep their relationships going. The high-functioning borderline woman provides the perfect foil for this "fatal attraction."

We now begin to comprehend more clearly the two levels at play in the narcissistic/borderline abusive couple. The narcissist, in his high-functioning states, is preoccupied with his own goals, his own efforts, his own achievements. His desire for a high-functioning career partner is an accompaniment to his own accomplishments and drive for perfection. The high-functioning borderline woman is searching for her male counterpart, one who has power and success and is ambitious enough to maintain both. What she does not realize is that what appears to be the very preoccupation needed to carve out success is the narcissist's preoccupation with self. In the narcissist is a baby who experienced a severe injury to his psychic self early in life and seeks adulation from others to mirror what has become his grandiose self. The borderline woman carries within herself a craving baby who brings into the relationship with the narcissist all her unmet frustrated needs. Not only do these needs become insatiable when they come up against the narcissist's self-involvement, they become persecutory. As much as this woman may despise her narcissistic partner's cruelty or sadistic tendencies, she will go to extremes to please him, often sexualizing the cruelty by making extensive self-sacrifices and by tolerating various forms of abuse out of her fear of being abandoned and unable to care for herself emotionally.

SEXUAL ACTING OUT IN THE DANCE

Two primary forms of sexual acting out occur in the abusive relationship between the narcissistic male and the high-functioning borderline female: one is adultery and impotence on the part of the narcissist; the other is adultery and frigidity on the part of the borderline. Despite the plethora of seemingly sophisticated sexual arrangements in our contemporary society, adultery is the most threatening type of acting out in a marriage. It is the ultimate betrayal of self, other, and marital vows. Further, the affair may be a diversional object (Lachkar 1992), that is, a defense against intimacy, an expression of hatred and cruelty toward the object.

In narcissistic/sadistic relations, the narcissistic adulterer cannot tolerate feelings of guilt and reparation. To own up to guilt is tantamount to owning up to imperfection. Instead, he willingly becomes the object of his partner's disdain and hatred. From his point of view, it is better to be despised than to face up to his own guilt. Yet, he is ready to drown his partner in guilt if she retaliates by also having an affair. Her imperfection, her disloyalty, is just the fodder the narcissist needs to re-establish his omnipotence and perfection.

A reverse form of adulterous acting out for the narcissist is impotence. Such impotence can be more destructive and painful than the affair because it signals the narcissist's withholding and withdrawal, creating in the borderline woman familiar and terrifying feelings of helplessness and desperation.

For the high-functioning borderline woman, an affair seems less of a threat to the relationship than her frigidity. Affairs serve in her search for tenderness, love, and involvement: any intimate relationship is better than none. On the other hand, her frigidity exposes her terror and hopelessness, her giving up the search; frigidity can therefore portend serious depression in the borderline woman.

Regardless of the forms of acting out assumed in the relationship between narcissistic abuser and his border-line partner, the power of the dance is hypnotic. Both partners become locked into their enactments to pre-serve their false selves, since long ago each renounced his or her true self. Despite their strivings to the contrary, neither believes that his or her true needs can be met. Let us turn now to two cases illustrating different renditions of this dance between narcissist and borderline.

CASE ILLUSTRATION:
THE "ENTITLED" NARCISSISTIC ABUSER

Ellen is a 34-year-old counselor at a private school. Her unresolved issues from childhood arouse an unconscious identificatory note within her unavailable, narcissistic boyfriend, who is a surgeon. We might speculate that a woman of this kind would have a keen sense of social consciousness and be sensitive and vulnerable to the responses and impressions of others. But Ellen, who needs to maintain her "status," loses this sensibility when she turns to her intimate relationship; she tolerates the demands and abuse from her narcissistic boyfriend. The very status she imagines as her salvation will prove to be the same status that leads to her psychic demise. The maintenance of her status image paradoxically anesthetizes her emotional state and, ultimately, her existence. Ellen's pathological attachment to a "tantalizing breast" (a father/boyfriend who promises the world, but does not follow through), is indicative of a number of female patients who are forever tormented by the rejecting or unavailable man.

Ellen: We have such difficulty communicating. Each time I bring up a problem, he acts as though I have just stabbed him in the chest. He personalizes everything, making it very difficult for me to tell him how I feel.

Bill: But you make impossible demands of me. You know I'm a surgeon, and that I don't have much time for you.

Ellen: You have time for everybody else. Besides, it's not just that. It's all the other stuff you do.

Bill: I resent her negativity. It just makes me feel like running away [narcissistic defense of withdrawal].

Ellen: And that's what you do! You run away!

Bill: She has no right to complain. I have given her everything. I take her on trips. I just took her skiing at St. Moritz. I buy her beautiful clothes. Show the therapist the gold watch I bought you!

Ellen: Yes, but each time we go on a trip, you invite all your friends or else you spend your whole time talking to them [his need for mirroring through "transportable" selfobjects]. We are never alone. Even when we go out to dinner or to the theater, I think, gee, this is great, we're going to have a nice romantic evening, and suddenly out of the blue his friends show up!

Bill: That doesn't happen all the time, and I resent you putting down my friends. I'm entitled to have my friends [excessive entitlement fantasies].

Ellen: Remember the last time we went to dinner and how none of your friends showed up? I was actually delighted. I thought finally we were going to have a nice quiet evening together. [to therapist] Now, let me tell you what happened—he disappeared. Bill went to the telephone and spent the whole time talking on the phone.

Therapist: How did you feel when Bill went to the telephone?

Ellen: Very abandoned, as if I didn't even exist [borderline annihilation fantasies].

Bill: Well, I had to check in on my surgeries.

Ellen: That's bullshit! You called your friends!

Bill: Look, the only time I have to be with my friends is on the weekends, so I don't understand why you have to be so jealous [projects into Ellen that it is bad to be jealous].

Ellen: I don't understand how I've dropped so far from being a high-functioning person to this desperate position. The administrators, the teachers, the students at my school all treat me with respect. Now I'm disorganized. I get throbbing headaches, I cry, I tremble easily. What has happened to me? Why do I feel so abused?

Therapist: Well, there is a part of you, Ellen, that's being abused. You feel neglected, mistreated, and ignored [validation of Ellen's experience]. Perhaps the main thing for us to understand is why you accept Bill's behavior and why you identify with the mistreatment.

Bill: (Laughing facetiously) Are you saying I'm abusing Ellen? Next, you'll be telling me I'm a child molester.

Therapist: Obviously, you're not that. You're not battering Ellen, but there is some form of abuse going on, and I believe you may also be feeling abused, Bill. [The therapist recalled to them that when they first made an appointment, they both mentioned feeling emotionally abused.]

Bill: You bet I do. Ellen is like my mother, very demanding, critical, and controlling. I feel like a prisoner.

Therapist: Tell me about your mother.

Bill: My mother would never allow me to do things my way. Not only my mother, but my grandmother who was even more controlling! They were always worried that I would make a mistake. To make a mistake was like a *shanda* [Yiddish word for "shame"].

Therapist: So you felt controlled and restricted [mirroring Bill's feelings].

Bill: I did. I felt like a prisoner.

Therapist: Now this relationship makes you feel like a prisoner. You feel criticized by Ellen, and Ellen feels criticized by you in the same way you were criticized by your mother, and you mistake Ellen's attempts to stand up to you as torture.

Ellen: That's kind of how it feels, as if he's a little kid fighting to get his way with his mother.

Bill: So why doesn't Ellen understand this? Doesn't she

know that I'm entitled to have my freedom and my space?

Therapist: This is confusing for you because what you were entitled to as a child is not the same kind of entitlement you can have as an adult, and when someone frustrates you, you feel tormented and suffocated [confronting the pathology, but empathic to the vulnerability].

Ellen: When he gets into all this entitlement stuff, I start to feel inadequate, as if I don't count. He's like my father who gave everyone else in the family attention.

Bill: I think this is getting too complicated. I told Ellen she should go and see someone else, a psychiatrist, someone with an M.D. degree.

Therapist: Now you're letting me know what it feels like to feel inadequate. Now I'm the inadequate therapist, not perfect enough [therapist opening up the space into the couple transference].

Ellen: I really like the way you didn't let Bill put you down just now. Bill always talks me out of my feelings, and when he does this, I begin to feel as though I don't exist. [Ellen is relieved at seeing how the therapist did not identify with Bill's attempt at debasement.]

Therapist: Ellen, I think you liked it because I didn't allow myself to identify with the suggestion of inadequacy. Although Bill doesn't have a right to belittle you, abandon you socially or emotionally, you need to understand there is a part of you that tends to identify with the negative projections. [Therapist is cautious to validate Ellen's experience of mistreatment before introducing her to her internal abuser, for example, a rejecting unavailable father amidst battling siblings.]

Ellen: That's true, because I feel as though I want to be treated like the rest of my friends. I want to get married. I want an engagement ring.

Bill: I told you we probably will get married, but I don't believe in engagement rings.

Therapist: Bill, you are trying to anesthetize Ellen, telling her she's not entitled to a ring, just as she tells you you're not entitled to your space, your freedom, or your friendships. For you, Ellen, when Bill denies your needs you lose your identity and forget who you are. [These interactions are typical of perverse relationships, whereby the focus is not on love but on domination and control.]

Bill: I don't know what I'm trying to do. I just want her to stop making all these demands on me!

Therapist: Anyway, we do need to stop now. All I can say is that every relationship makes demands, has pressure, as does this therapeutic relationship [couple transference]. But I worry. You, Bill, may feel the demands for commitment here may lead to pressure and torture. Ellen, you may worry that I will abandon you, especially when I'm being empathic with Bill. So

I don't think these feelings occur only within the relationship. They are beginning to happen here too. With this in mind, we'll continue with this. See you both next time.

DISCUSSION

This case brings up many technical problems. First, how does one show empathy to Bill while also standing up against the abuse of Ellen? Further, how does the therapist show empathy to Ellen without causing more narcissistic injury to Bill? It is essential that the therapist acknowledge Ellen's subjective experience that she does feel abused and mistreated by Bill, verifying her experience through appropriate mirroring and empathy. However, this may be in direct conflict with the therapist's ability to act as a "hard enough object." Frances Tustin's notion of the "hard object" (1981) corresponds to this line of inquiry in that the more disturbed child needs firm protective objects to stand up against in order to feel safe.

The therapist must confront the couple about the emotional abuse while simultaneously providing the function of the mirroring mother in her reflection of their feeling states (Ellen's sense of being neglected; Bill's feeling imprisoned). Countertransference issues and tension in the therapist can lead to a serious sabotage of the treatment. In cases like this one, some therapists who are not M.D.s might feel discomfited and defensive when confronted with the implication the patient made that they are limited and inadequate. It is important to understand Bill's put-down of the therapist as his transference issue, within the context of the "couple transference" (Lachkar 1992). For Bill, the put-down was a projection into the therapist of his own critical mother and grandmother. For Ellen, the therapist's response became an opportunity to envision how she might, like the therapist, stop identifying with Bill's projections.

From a technical point of view, the therapist must, without losing neutrality, act with deftness, acknowledging the abuse but not dwelling on it. To do more than acknowledge its existence runs the risk of getting caught up in blame and shame enactments, thus replicating the original narcissistic injury. Rather, the therapist needs to focus on the narcissist's experience, in this case, exploring with Bill how he also might be feeling abused. This approach leads to deeper insights, such as Bill's tendency to distort and project his anxiety into Ellen, and Ellen's tendency to fuse and identify with Bill's projections. Showing the partners that they are both in the abuse provides a dual benefit. First, it validates each of their needs and perceptions, and second, it promotes a willingness in both of them to engage in introspection.

The therapist introduces the notion of the couple transference as she addresses how each experiences deprivation within the therapeutic domain. The common denominator is deprivation, which becomes the heart of the dual projective identifications. Both the aggressor and the victim feel deprived, as each plays out his or her own subjective experience. The aggressor transforms his deprivation by disposing his needs onto the victim. The victim absorbs and identifies with the negative projections, turning normal dependency needs into self-hatred and self-effacement. In the couple transference, the elements of deprivation are reproduced as they get projected onto the therapist.

CASE ILLUSTRATION:
THE FEMALE NARCISSISTIC ABUSER

There are many instances when men feel emotionally abused. The following case illustrates this type of violation. Samantha is an insatiable woman who never seems to have enough, a female narcissistic abuser who feels overly entitled. Because of her early deprivation, she feels free to use men, playing out exaggerated fantasies of entitlement.

Tony, a young architect, called for an appointment out of desperation, fearing that his wife was "screwing" other men again. He felt manipulated by Samantha and said he was at his wits' end. He described his wife as an extraordinary beauty, a knockout, with "gorgeous tits" and body.

When I first met Samantha, I saw a tall, rather

anorexic forty-nine-year-old woman, with large breasts that looked like implants, long porcelain fingernails, and long, stringy, dyed greenish-blond hair. She was wearing a leopard skin unitard and five-inch high heels.

Samantha: I didn't come to talk about us, Tony. I'm really here for myself. I think I should be seeing my own therapist, because [as she turned to me] I don't know why I waste my time with Tony. Tony is not the man of my dreams.

Tony: This is how she talks to me. I feel like smashing her.

Samantha: I do need to see a therapist.

Tony: She always makes me feel like a nothing. I feel jacked around and am in so much pain. I've had it with this woman.

Samantha: Look, I love Tony. We have great sex and passion together. It's better than anyone. I feel good with Tony.

Therapist: How important is Tony to you, Samantha?

Samantha: It's never enough. I always want more.

Tony: Like your shoes?

Samantha: Oh, he's talking about my shoes. You know, I have over five hundred pairs of shoes.

Therapist: Five hundred pairs?

Samantha: That's my thing, shoes. I just love shoes. Even though clothes are important and I do have beautiful clothes, shoes are my thing.

Therapist: But none of those things feels like enough?

Tony: Right now she has another man. This is what ticks me off.

Samantha: Well, he's not like an ordinary man. He's more like a daddy, a sugar daddy. He buys me things. He would do anything for me in a pinch. But I don't love him the way I love Tony.

Therapist: Samantha, are you aware that this might be painful for Tony? [Tony leaves the room to go outside to smoke.]

Samantha: [Secretly whispering to therapist] Look, I have a problem. Tony isn't Jewish.

[Tony returns.]

Therapist: I guess it's difficult to face that all relationships have limitations, that no one can have it all: the shoes, all the clothes, all the affairs, all the money. Just as I can't have all the patients [attempt to bond]. You both seem to be suffering. [To Samantha] I believe it's hard for you to imagine that having all these affairs while married to Tony is hurtful, and is a betrayal not only to him but to yourself. Especially to that hurt, deprived little girl inside. So you do a little dance. You play out this deprivation again and again. "If Daddy loves me, he will buy me shoes and I'm really special. If Daddy doesn't love me, and if I'm not special, he won't buy me shoes." So you need lots of daddies to make you feel special and appreciated, but in the end you feel empty, angry, and unfulfilled.

You feel frustrated because this doesn't feed your soul. As you play this out, you re-create the scenario of a little girl who is insatiable, and not the independent woman that you are.

Tony: I feel so jerked around.

Therapist: Well, it's not just that you *feel* jerked around, you *are* being jerked around. The healthy side of you is not willing to put up with this and is asking for help.

Tony: I feel abused.

Samantha: [Laughs] Abused? Now I'm an abuser!

Therapist: Samantha, you do have legitimate needs, but you don't know which needs those are or how to get them met. You think you need shoes and lots of men, but those cannot meet your real needs. Instead of facing things inside yourself that are painful, you get rid of those feelings by projecting them into Tony. Then, he becomes the needy one, and you are home free. What you haven't realized is that you are needy, and it's good to be needy, good to be dependent, and you don't have to get rid of these feelings. The important thing is that both of you are hurting, and you each need help.

Samantha: Well, I have good reason to feel deprived. Even though my parents gave me everything, they never spent time with me. My father was always working. We had butlers, maids, chauffeurs, but I never spent time with my dad. He just bought me lots of things. I need men. I love men! When I don't have one I find another or else I keep them at the same time!

Tony: I'm sick of this game.

Therapist: This is not a game, Tony. Neither of you is in a position to take care of your own needs right now, let alone take care of one another's. For now, the reality is that you are in this relationship, and we need to continue to see what evolves out of our work together.

Samantha: Sounds okay with me.

Tony: Can we meet again?

Therapist: Yes, with pleasure. How about the same time next week?

Samantha and Tony: See you then.

DISCUSSION

During the course of treatment, Samantha remembered that after her younger sister was born, she tried to regain her father's attention by throwing her shoes away under the pretense of being unable to walk. The shoes served as a symbolic representation of the father who withdrew his attention from her and toward her new sibling.

Because of Samantha's lack of sensitivity to Tony's needs, feelings of rage and sadistic responses were evoked in him (the attachment to a rejecting internal object). Although Tony never became violent with Samantha, one could understand his rageful responses toward her.

Samantha had a delusional sense of entitlement and a grandiose fantasy that by seeing other men she would make up for her "lost father." The therapist's intervention gave the couple a sense of what happened to each of them when Samantha engaged in the delusional fantasy, that is, when she went looking for the "lost father." This enactment came from her primitive paranoid-schizoid position, whereby she re-enacted the fantasy rather than being able to work it through. This is a far cry from what happens in the depressive position, where one reaches the realization that one cannot make up for the loss by replacing the object; instead, one first must deal with the loss of the object. Many clinicians fail to understand the reason for reparation or the need to work through the depressive position. As Klein (1940) reminds us, if one fails to mourn, one does not develop the capacity to get in contact with needs.

The relationship between Samantha and Tony is of the parasitic dependency type. Tony is a borderline personality with masochistic features, and Samantha is a severely narcissistic woman who forms perverse relationships. Samantha cannot tolerate any frustration and so substitutes physical possessions and multiple intimate relationships for healthy dependency needs. Such women induce severe feelings of worthlessness in their mates. For Tony, identifying with Samantha's projections made him "feel like a nothing," and thus evoked his impulse to attack, invade, and emotionally live inside his mate. He would say, "If I'm good Samantha will love me, and if I'm bad she won't." Tony's object choice exhibits an attachment to a non-available internal mother who continually taunts him.

TREATMENT

Each personality type described in this book has her or his own idiosyncratic nature in terms of how s/he responds to various therapeutic interventions and interpretations. The kinds of interpretations we give to a narcissist, then, are qualitatively different than the ones we give to a borderline, a passive-aggressive, or a schizoid. The narcissist lives within an omnipotent world, filled with fantasies of perfection and excessive entitlement wishes. How different this is from a borderline's inner world, which is filled with depths of despair, fear of falling into black holes, and persistent anticipatory/persecutory anxieties that cause her to cling desperately to whatever object she can find. While the qualitative differences are not absolute for each disorder, and despite there being a carryover between disorders, there are some general guidelines that are useful for us to consider. A more thorough explication of treatment phases and techniques is available in Chapter 8.

In treating the narcissistic abuser, the most difficult

task for the therapist is to explore and examine the narcissist's omnipotence without losing the patient. The dilemma is to find just the right moment to mirror back the narcissist's original injury by saying something like, "It seems as though it is very difficult for you to take in any help from me, because when you do, you feel small and less than perfect." This must be done with care. We do not want to diminish the narcissist's creative talents, or eliminate his persistent drive or motivation, while we are endeavoring to gradually decrease both his omnipotence and omniscience.

Narcissists deny their need for help and have unrealistic, grandiose expectations of the treatment. "Give me a diagnosis! Tell me what the outcome will be! How long do I need to keep coming here!" Modell (1976) has called the creation of the narcissist's cocoon an "impregnable fortress."

In this cocoon, the patient tries to maintain the illusion that he can nourish himself, needing nothing from the therapist because he is omnipotently self-sufficient.

Because of the narcissist's tendency to fight or withdraw, the most important first step for the therapist is to bond with the narcissist. A borderline victim, on the other hand, will be content for a while just to be present in the therapy as long as she knows her own therapeutic bonding is imminent. The borderline will initially feel soothed by the therapist's presence, by feeling that someone cares enough to consider her inner world. Eventually, the borderline will be able to make use of the therapist as someone who confronts the abuse. But for the narcissist, the therapeutic path can only be carved out by mirroring and introspection. The narcissist will withdraw from the therapeutic alliance if he does not feel appreciated, or if he senses any possible injury to the self, or that his entrapment fantasies might be realized.

In treatment, a narcissist often acts as though the therapist does not exist, except as a mirror of his specialness. He may feel entitled to withdraw if his sense of grandiosity is in any way impinged upon, such as when his excessive demands to change appointment times are not met, or if the therapist herself needs to change the time. What is supportive of the therapy at such moments is if at least the narcissist is consciously aware of, and overtly expresses, his entitlement fantasies. This provides the therapist with the opportunity to address and explore these fantasies with the patient.

With the narcissistic abuser we must focus also on guilt, a psychic experience from which he will want to withdraw. For the narcissist to face guilt he must face imperfection in the self, which in turn creates overwhelming feelings of vulnerability. However, when the therapist can link the facing of guilt with the narcissist's power, then the narcissist might be willing to begin exploring what is for him treacherous territory. When the therapist suggests, "What's wrong with feeling remorse for your act? It's normal to feel appropriate guilt and to want to repair the damage. If you continue to run away, you will also run away from the true part of your nature," the narcissist may consider for the first time that there could be a potential benefit in not fleeing. The narcissist has the perverted sense that to be grandiose and omnipotent is good and to be dependent and needy is bad. He will need to learn from the therapeutic exchange that omnipotence does not enhance love, it destroys it and is its greatest enemy.

There is a delicate balancing act to be achieved in working with the narcissistic abuser and his borderline partner. The borderline may perceive the therapist's empathic mirroring of the narcissist as weakness. After all, it is through similar attempts that the borderline woman has been trying to win over her narcissistic partner. Borderline women fall in love easily with unavailable men. They cling to these men for life support and will sacrifice their integrity and personal power in order to please them. They may also use their seductiveness to achieve a sense of power but this quickly fails because they lack the feelings of entitlement of the narcissist.

The borderline woman tends to diminish her own importance in pursuit of the relationship with the narcissist. Because of a profound sense of shame she will repudiate her femininity as well as her needs. This accounts for her propensity toward masochism and self-sacrifice. She will convert this propensity into very concrete terms: "If I'm good, he will love me; if I'm bad, he will ignore or leave me." According to Bach (1994), "the narcissistic sadist denies his object needs by overvaluing the importance of his drive discharge, whereas the narcissistic masochist denies his drive needs by overemphasizing the importance of object attachments" (p. 18).

Once the therapeutic alliance has been established, the therapist can then introduce both of the partners to their internal abusers by incorporating the notion of their dual projective identifications. Only after both abuser and victim have been sufficiently bathed in empathy, mirroring, listening, holding, and validation can they carefully shift into examining the dual projective identification process. Through bonding and weaning, the therapist begins to describe how each partner participates in the "dance of abuse." As the borderline partner accepts and incorporates the negative projections, the more needy, demanding, self-destructive, and insatiable she becomes. The withdrawing narcissist evokes "rejected child" fantasies in his borderline partner, and this rejected child then becomes the demanding baby, triggering unbearable feelings of dependency in the narcissist, which cause him to withdraw further. By identifying this interaction, the therapist is able to bond with the borderline not by disavowing the borderline's needs, but by demonstrating for the narcissist how he projects his healthy dependency as a form of evacuation to rid the psyche of what is felt to be intolerable. Thus, the dance goes on.

The high-functioning, borderline woman will eventually feel more in control as she realizes that the abuse is not only played out externally. Once she learns how to manage the internal abuser she will feel more in control and in contact with her true self. The idea that she has remained unconsciously loyal to the internal abuser is a foreign one: she may feel insulted, wounded, or even betrayed by the therapist. But as she makes more contact with these internal abusers, they become "abuser friendly" and she is able to embrace her true needs and meet some of them herself. A surge of excitement will surface as she captures the difference between inner and outer reality. Her desperate clinging to the narcissist partner will gradually diminish as she learns how to manage her intrapsychic and emotional life.

As the narcissist becomes aware of his own internal abusers—the harsh, critical, ever more demanding internal objects he has carried inside him throughout his life—he will learn not to project these into his borderline partner. Concurrently, her easing up of her insatiable demands will show him some space to consider feeling his own needs for intimacy.

Once all this happens, the therapist will know progress is being made. At this point, the therapist as a real person who has a contribution to make will be invited into the couple transference, and a new therapeutic space will open up.

In treating an abusive couple we must not forget that such treatment is not only about pain and conflict, but about opposing needs. It is also about love and strength and courage. Each partner has positive attributes, which is how they have been able to become high functioning and successful in certain areas of their lives. These strengths, which function as false-self strengths when they are geared toward fulfilling false-self needs, will convert to true-self strengths as each partner begins to function out of his and her true-self needs.

๛ 4 ๛

The Borderline Abuser

I was Ms. Independent who in a few months had let myself become utterly dependent on that man. Before, I felt strong, I had direction in my life. Now, I feel as if I have been poisoned with some toxic substance. Whatever I do, he makes me feel that I'm not good enough. This makes me try harder, but even then, I'm never enough for him. Why can't I leave?

THE BORDERLINE

In the previous chapter, we examined the dynamics intrinsic to the narcissistic abuser and his borderline partner. Now let us look at the reverse: the borderline abuser and his narcissistic intimate. The borderline is one who does not have a sense of self and thus suffers from chronic feelings of emptiness accompanied by profound fears of annihilation, abandonment, and separation and persecutory anxiety.

Unable to utilize selfobjects (Kohut 1971, 1977), the borderline exhibits a deficiency in the capacity to bond and has an impaired ability to think or learn from experience (Bion 1962). In search of psychic relief, borderlines unconsciously evacuate parts of themselves into others, translocating the self via the projective identification process. It is this very process, however, that further weakens the self, which leads to a variety of maladaptive configurations including psychosomatic illnesses, and such damaging behaviors as bingeing, self-mutilation, and suicide attempts. Many borderlines have described the experience as, "I feel as though I'm going to jump out of my skin."

Borderlines evoke in their partners a defective sense of self as the latter identify with the borderlines' projections. Thus, borderlines "live" only by projecting their intolerable mental and emotional contents inside the psychic space of their intimate others. This unbearable state of being causes them to vanish psychically. Carrying a depleted sense of self, they do not feel deserving of attention or love and compensate for this by being willing to do almost anything to feel some level of bonding or relatedness. Borderlines frequently have retaliatory fantasies toward their "depriving" partners—fantasies that they are prone to act out. Even after a separation or divorce, the borderline may spend the rest of his life getting even in order to maintain some sense of connectedness. Retaliation becomes a more pervasive force than life itself (Lachkar 1984, 1992). Their daily experience of poor reality-testing and impaired judgment creates a painful mix of difficulties with self-regulation, impulse control, and limit setting or adhering to others' limits. Borderlines are almost completely devoid of the capacity for self-soothing, empathy, and the ability to affirm themselves (see Manfield 1992), except in self-defensive ways. Unlike the narcissist, who will withdraw when injured, the borderline either fuses or attacks when injured and responds with shame and blame defenses.

Typically, borderlines have been emotionally abandoned early in life by parents who were absent, alcoholic, abusive, or emotionally unavailable. Being easy targets for the negative projections of others casts them in the perpetual role of victim through maintaining the cycle of abusive relationships. They remain forever loyal to the allegorical world of lost mothers, lost fathers, and abandoned babies. Because of the excruciating shame, they fear that if real needs and desires are expressed, they will be ridiculed or rejected. Their insatiable yearning for relatedness causes them to bond with their partners through pain. It's much easier to feel connected to pain than to have to deal with real needs and desires.

In this captivity, the experience of the internal world is felt to be ominous, with mysterious and foreboding forces lurking in the shadows. One borderline patient dreamed that he was spinning at his sports club. As he touched the lockers they turned to gold (his real needs), and suddenly below him stood a dark, horrific figure hiding in the basement. Through dreams we see the wisdom of the unconscious. Borderline patients often have delusional fantasies about introspection, but when they do seek inward, as in this dream, quite the opposite appears—the gold.

How does shame fit within the schemata of the borderline personality disorder, and how does it relate to dependency needs? And further, to the topic of abuse? Shame has only recently resurfaced as a major psychological dynamic. Although Klein (1957) only briefly refers to shame, it is alluded to throughout her work as it relates to envy, greed, and persecutory anxiety (Grotstein and Mason, personal communication 1996). Shame is part object functioning, as opposed to guilt, which is whole object functioning, and which operates at a higher level of the superego.

Lansky (1987, 1995) describes shame as a matter between the person and his group or society, while guilt is primarily a matter between a person and his conscience. Shame juxtaposes the borderline's needs against his sense of humiliation and terror for having needs. An important component of this shame is persecutory anxiety, producing within the borderline a fragmented position and the terror of falling into a psychic void. Since shame is associated with anticipatory anxiety and annihilation fantasies, it must either be spilt off or projected.

Klein (1957) makes an important distinction between envy and jealousy, considering envy to be the more primitive and fundamental emotion, one that exhausts external objects and seeks to destroy. Envy is not based on love but is a two-part process: in the first part the subject, who feels like a nothing, embodies the other with being an everything; in the second part, the subject wishes to destroy the other because s/he cannot tolerate the need for the idealized object. Envy is destructive because as the subject craves and yearns for what the other has (the breast), s/he simultaneously loathes it. Because s/he cannot tolerate the states of dependency necessary for attainment, s/he is left always object seeking but never object finding. In order to survive the enemy and its concomitant need to destroy the object of desire, the borderline must either split off these destructive feelings or project them into others.

THE BORDERLINE ABUSER

My experience as both clinician and supervisor has provided substantial clinical data to support the notion that the male borderline personality is the most prevalent perpetrator of physical or emotional abuse. The reasons for this are threefold. First, the borderline shows a clear proclivity toward primitive defenses (splitting, projection, projective identification, magical thinking, omnipotent denial). Since he exhibits poor reality testing and impulse control, he makes poor choices in partners, forming parasitic bonds.

Second, in severely disturbed relationships, the borderline's love feelings intersect with aggression, unconsciously converting love into a malignant experience. In general, the borderline is one who fuses with mother's body and thus typically confuses sexuality and bonding with (m)other's body. Sexuality linked with perversion becomes the replacement for love. The primitive nature of the personality organization of borderline patients shows marked tendencies toward aggression. Because many borderlines experience themselves as victims of other people's aggression, they tenaciously rationalize their own aggression. With little tolerance for ambivalence, frustration, and confusion, these patients show alternating fluctuations of masochistic and sadistic tendencies, turning first against the self, and then against the other (Kernberg 1990, 1992).

Third, borderlines, especially those who have developed some level of a false self or an "as if" personality, will initially comply, then explode suddenly. In perceiving a threat (usually not accurately), they will lash out in retaliation. This characteristic is what makes the borderline abusive. It is this sudden shift from false self functioning to the experience of being flooded by the other that leads to impulsive acts: "I just couldn't take it anymore. I let her have it!"

THE HIGH-FUNCTIONING PARTNERS OF BORDERLINE ABUSERS

Conflict is ever-present in even benign borderline/ narcissistic relationships. These opposed personality types have many distorted views about the nature of healthy and unhealthy dependency needs. Through their unconscious evacuations and projections into the other, they mold to each other's psychopathologies. The borderline's envy and overwhelming need for relatedness, combined with boundary diffusion and lack of impulse control, draw him to the overly entitled, narcissistic, high-functioning woman who appears to "have it all." Additionally, since the borderline does not believe he is lovable or deserving, he is impelled to pursue someone who keeps him forever connected to the non-deserving rejected self. For a while, the borderline can act at being the perfect mirroring object for the narcissist, but because of his inability to contain or sustain either self or other (Lachkar 1984, 1997), the borderline cannot fulfill the promise.

What causes anxiety for the borderline is not the same as what causes anxiety for the narcissist, and this qualitative difference is essential not only in making diagnostic distinctions but in offering appropriate therapeutic responses. For the borderline, inner turmoil and confusion torment the psyche; such chaos appears to be absent in the narcissist. For the narcissist, her archaic dependency needs evoke the greatest anxiety. With the borderline's impaired sense of self, he becomes the ideal recipient for the narcissist's projection of her faulty parts, allowing her to maintain her grandiose and perfect self. The narcissistic, high-functioning woman is attracted to the borderline's apparent selflessness and availability (because he has split off his needs), and his willingness to do almost anything to receive the relatedness he desires. These aspects within the borderline emanate from his envy and basic sense of shame, and provide the narcissist, at least in the beginning, with pretense of a perfect mirroring object.

THE BORDERLINE/NARCISSISTIC DANCE

In the psychological dance between the borderline and the narcissist, when the borderline mirrors, the narcissist thrives. In the abusive enactments, when the borderline attacks, the narcissist withdraws. The narcissist's appearance of not needing the other justifies the borderline's intensified demands for intimacy, thus compelling the narcissist to withdraw even further. Obsessed with guilt for abandoning the borderline, the narcissist is wooed back with the borderline's perfunctory vow, "I'll do anything, I'll be anything you want me to be, just don't leave!" Seduced by the borderline's promises and his own need to be mirrored, the narcissist returns only to find that once again, the promises are meaningless. Inevitably, the borderline abuser controls his narcissistic partner through impulsive expressions of uncontrollable rage. The borderline's sudden acts of desperation confirm the narcissistic woman's defense of distancing, the belief that intimacy is bad and dangerous and that one is better off living disconnected from dependency. With her subsequent withdrawal, the narcissist invariably fulfills the borderline's worst fears and adds to his already present sense of shame.

In their "relational dance" (see Lachkar 1992), the narcissist's tendency to withdraw stirs up the borderline's most profound anxiety: an abandonment he must prevent at any cost. Yet, while the narcissistic woman may withdraw or flee, she will return to the borderline in order to be mirrored and admired. The borderline cannot be freed from his unceasing efforts to prove his existence and so provides his narcissistic partner with the special sense of her own existence. As bad as the pain is for each partner, it is still preferable to the void, the "black hole," and the meaninglessness that epitomizes their inner states of terror (Grotstein 1990).

And so, the dance goes on and on.

CASE ILLUSTRATION:
THE BORDERLINE "PACK RAT"

Joanna: Michael was absolutely out of control. He got so enraged with Jonathan [Joanna's son, Michael's stepson], complaining about his messy room. Michael then dumped all my son's socks and toys on the floor. You should have seen Michael: his veins became enlarged, and his eyes looked as if they were going to pop out of their sockets.

Michael: I was only trying to keep some order [over-whelmed by his inner chaos].

Joanna: But you should have seen the look on your face. You looked like a serial killer. You wouldn't stop. You were relentless. Then you began to pick on the maid, referring to her as a stupid peasant woman who didn't know how to clean.

Therapist: [To Michael] Last week we were talking about the difficulty you have throwing out things and possessions.

Michael: But that stuff is important to me.

Joanna: Well, other stuff is important to me. It's important that you make room for us, for me and for Jonathan. You're the one who wanted to get married and have us live with you. You promised before we were married that you would make space for us, but there's no room. Everything is cluttered with your possessions. How many people do we know who save used washers?

Michael: [Laughing] Well, it's true, I don't like to throw out anything. I'm a collector.

Joanna: A collector? Of what? Junk? [To therapist] Michael is a pack rat. His possessions get in the way of us being a normal family. Instead of taking walks with us, spending time with Jonathan, he sits there working at his computer in a pile of rubble. What galls me is how can he expect my son to be neat when Michael is such a slob. Other people never treat me this way. I don't know why I put up with this from Michael. This morning, he screamed about his shirts not being ironed correctly.

Therapist: You're not used to being treated this way.

Joanna: You bet. In my office, there is no way I would tolerate this chaos and this confusion. Nothing would ever get accomplished. I don't know why I put up with this at home.

Therapist: Michael, I notice you've been very quiet.

Michael: There's nothing I can say. Anything I say, I know she'll get angry with me. I just want peace, and I don't like being harassed.

Therapist: When your "peace" is disrupted, it might make you feel messy and pressured inside. So you defend against these anxious feelings by trying to clean up others, or by holding onto possessions. Your possessions take the place of intimacy, which is another "messy" need.

Joanna: Is that why I always feel so much pressure when I'm with Michael?

Therapist: Perhaps there is a part of you, Joanna, that identifies with this messy side and fears it, so you try to maintain the perfect side of you, the corporate side of you at home.

Michael: I don't follow any of this.

Joanna: See, he never wants to talk about anything, and, of course, he never *knows* what I'm talking about either.

Therapist: Michael, I think you are fearful that if we explore some of these feelings it will create even more of a mess. If we can talk about your feelings, you will not have to act them out in destructive ways.

Michael: When I was little, there was an earthquake and I lost all of my possessions.

Therapist: That must have been very distressing. Does it feel like another kind of earthquake when Joanna intrudes on your things?

Michael: I really don't want to bother with this. Therapy is just a waste of my time. I'm very busy. I have a court case tomorrow, and I have a brief to finish.

Therapist: Are you telling me how uncomfortable intimacy makes you feel?

Michael: Okay, I'll try and make it next week.

Joanna: I will definitely be here. Thank you.

DISCUSSION

Michael is a borderline "abuser" who is not looking for perfection in himself but is projecting his ego ideal into Joanna and Jonathan, expecting them to be perfect. Because of his relentless demands and excessive complaints, he ends up provoking Joanna to view him precisely as he does not want to be seen: as the chaotic and confused person he is. As a pack rat, Michael demonstrates how closely aligned he still is to his mother's body and how unable he is to separate. Joanna and her son (and eventually the therapist) become the invading oedipal rivals: the dangerous outsiders who intrude upon this fantasized symbiotic bond. Michael's clutter is a reflection of his messy internal world, which obviates intimacy and healthy dependency (Michael's loyalty to his idealized internal mother). Michael has a delusional sense that his "droppings" are golden pieces for mother to admire. These non-gratifying objects eventually transform into anal objects, which constrict and restrain his emotional life. His feelings and needs live inside a tight anal hole, a rat hole.

Michael finds it extremely difficult living with another person. No one is allowed to touch his "droppings," for fear it would destroy him or contaminate another person. Joanna, on the other hand, cannot tolerate a less than perfect environment, just as she cannot tolerate a less than perfect self. Michael's promise to "create space" for her and her son is understood unconsciously by her as an implicit agreement to mirror her perfection, not her own intolerably messy, archaic needs. By disowning these needs, she assumes Michael will contain them. When he cannot, she is thrown into an emotional collision with them, one that she is unable to manage, except by throwing everything out indiscriminately.

Here we see Joanna's desperate attempts to rid herself of anything that is tainted or imperfect. While her desire for a clean and orderly home is not unreasonable, she has found in Michael the perfect mate upon whom to project her early and unacceptable needs and then to reject them in him.

CASE ILLUSTRATION: MR. AND MRS. D.

The case of Mr. and Mrs. D. not only portrays what transpires in the beleaguered relationship between a borderline abuser and his high-functioning, narcissistic wife, but also serves as an example of working within the couple transference. Mrs. D. shows a higher level of functioning than her borderline husband. As Mr. D. resorts to more primitive defenses to fuse with and then destroy the object, she operates at a higher level of superego functioning while withholding herself from the object.

Mr. D., a 50-year-old, attractive, well-dressed engineer, initiated treatment complaining of marital difficulties. He stated that his wife is sexually unavailable, and withholds time, attention, and affection. Mrs. D., the narcissistic wife, is a 40-year-old, pretty, slim, and impeccably dressed schoolteacher. They had been married for ten years and had two children. Mr. D. was seen on an individual basis until Mrs. D. was "invited" into treatment, which is when conjoint treatment began. The couple therapy continued over a period of a year and a half along with concomitant individual psychotherapy sessions for each.

Mr. D. was an only child whose father died when he

was 10 years old and whose mother was an alcoholic. His mother remarried but divorced shortly thereafter. Although Mr. D. did have relationships with males in his formative years, he unconsciously blamed his mother for his father's death and his subsequent poor male bonding experiences. He felt very insecure about his role as husband and father, identifying with his helpless mother. At first, he was thought to be an obsessive-compulsive personality, but upon further exploration, revealed a typical borderline personality structure.

In the months before treatment began, Mr. D. had become unable to maintain a full erection, although he claimed he was never impotent before. This failure was felt as a severe blow to his self-esteem and produced intense anxiety within him. In addition, he expressed growing resentment toward his wife, and had difficulty taking any stand with her or expressing any desire or need. Simultaneously, he complained about his wife's withholding of sex, blaming her for his impotence and fearing that one day she would banish him. He believed that they had had a good marriage in the early days before his wife began to reject him. Now, "all she expects is for me to pay the bills," he confided.

In the early sessions of the therapy, Mr. D. wanted to blame his wife. All attempts to address the issue of his own internal world were to no avail. His response to the therapy induced in the therapist powerful countertrans-ference reactions, causing her to offer quick remedies for his overwhelming anxiety. When these quick fix solutions proved ineffective, he would have intense and sudden outbursts. He began demanding that his wife participate in the therapy, an apparent replication of his demands for her to have sex. He worried that his attempt to have his wife join him in therapy would end up as fruitless as asking her for sex. On an unconscious level, Mr. D. was enacting the helpless, impotent mother role, projecting into his spouse his "bad" dependency needs, which were then met with rebuffs. The therapist, failing in her efforts at prompting Mr. D. to deal with his internal issues, succumbed to his wishes, and invited the wife to join the therapy.

In the borderline/narcissistic couple, it is the borderline who typically seeks help, as narcissists rarely offer themselves willingly to marital treatment, believing in their own perfection. Mrs. D. did agree to come to some sessions but felt that the problems in the marriage had nothing to do with her and hoped that her attendance would facilitate her husband's improvement. In Mrs. D.'s opinion, the problems began soon after the wedding when Mr. D.'s desire for intimacy gradually diminished. She felt he did the opposite of what she requested: "If I asked him to rub my back, he would pinch or pull at me. He hurt me, so of course I withdrew." She revealed that she no longer wanted to have sex with him because he was insensitive when they had sex, almost as if he hurt her "on purpose."

Mrs. D. described her mother as very domineering, religious, and rejecting, and her father as passive and detached. She recalled being the special child until her baby brother was born, and felt at his birth that she had been dethroned. Mrs. D. was left with deep feelings of loss: "I spent the rest of my life trying to prove to my parents how perfect I was, and I would do anything for their attention." This loss became an unforgettable narcissistic injury, from which she had no opportunity to recover. She recounted how her mother never supported her burgeoning femininity, but favored her brother. So she became "a tomboy," eschewing dolls. "Eventually, I learned I didn't need anyone. Even when I got my period, my mother ignored me and never offered any help or advice, or showed any concern."

Mr. D.'s poor male identification made him feel uncertain about his role as a husband and father, whereas Mrs. D. suffered similar problems in her gender identification. Ultimately, she had disidentified with her mother and fused with her father by taking on his cold and detached ways—ways which would become intolerable for her needy and insecure husband.

DISCUSSION

In their "dance," Mrs. D. became the "dead" parent whom Mr. D. tried desperately to revive. Similarly, Mrs. D. took on the role of his unavailable mother, intoxicated with her own self-absorption. Mr. D.'s needs became the "disgusting" split-off part of his wife's original dependency, the part of her that yearned for a special place with the unavailable parent(s). In this scenario, Mr. D.'s "normal" requests for sex felt instead like hurtful rebukes of Mrs. D.'s existence. Mrs. D. projected her infantile guilt (she must have been responsible for not being appealing enough to "hold" her parents when they had another child) into Mr. D., which then ignited his shame (persecutory anxiety emanating from the delusion that dependency is dangerous and disgusting). Conversely, Mr. D. projected his envy and shame into Mrs. D., which induced in her a guilt-ridden self so unbearable that she had to react with harsh judgments and withdrawal: dependency meant being less than perfect, and femininity too was a sign of imperfection.

As the "dance" developed, we saw Mr. D. fusing with his mother's/wife's body, living within her psychically. His sexualization often involved sadism (the pinching and hurting). In this early stage of the therapy, Mrs. D. continued to rebuff Mr. D.'s sexual advances, inducing in him increased desperation and neediness: "If only she would not withhold from me, I would feel more like a person. She makes me feel as if I don't even exist."

As the therapy advanced, there was an opening of the therapeutic space as bonding developed with the therapist. Both partners began to tolerate the "not knowing," some preliminary giving up of "memory and desire" (Bion

1967, p. 143). The therapist took on a more active role, using both confrontation and management. The major shift for Mrs. D. was in her willingness to consider giving up her omnipotence and her all-knowing attitude ("I just know what he's going to do and say."). Actually, Mrs. D. was quite relieved to find that this understanding gave her *more* control in the relationship, not less. During the next few months, Mrs. D. began to feel some assurance in her newly acquired sense of being a feminine person, the result of her preliminary identification with the therapist's qualities of sensitivity and vulnerability. Her developing capacities to tolerate her own imperfections and those of her husband (e.g., she could get mad at him instead of projecting into him and then rejecting him) contributed greatly to her feelings of increased security and the knowledge that the marriage was of paramount importance to her.

As his wife was more receptive to him and committed to their relationship, it came as quite a shock to Mr. D. that he was not so much interested in intimacy and making love as he was in using sex as an act of aggression (the perverse use of love) against his passive, self-involved mother/wife. He began to comprehend his own true dependency needs, and as he and his wife learned to appreciate one another's vulnerabilities, they exhibited an increased capacity for abstract thinking: to think about their feelings and needs instead of acting them out. Each sensed a desire within the other for reparation. Mr. D. became more able to tolerate ambiguity, the notion of many forces operating simultaneously. He also learned that he did not have to "abuse," "seduce," or demand; he could ask. Gradually, Mr. D. realized that his striving for bonding transcended sex, and that sex for him was a substitute for emotional contact and responsiveness.

In the final phase of treatment, Mrs. D. observed how her underlying fears of deficiency not only related to the difficulties in her marriage but impacted every area of her life, including her career and her children. Her defenses of withdrawal and isolation gave her a false sense of power, but ultimately kept her unprotected in a hostile internal, and sometimes external, world. With the therapist, Mrs. D.'s desire for special treatment still manifested itself in several ways, such as insistence on fee reduction or on changing hours to suit her schedule. There were times it would appear that Mrs. D. would never be able to take in nourishment: she knew it all, had all the answers. When the therapist brought up important issues, she was seen as the "agenda" mother; when she was more silent and reflective, she was being the passive, impotent father.

But all in all, the therapy proved effective. Both Mr. D. and Mrs. D. came to realize that expressing and responding to their true needs could enhance their relationship. In time, the conjoint sessions ended with Mrs. D.'s requesting to see the therapist in individual sessions, and Mr. D.'s requesting a referral to a male therapist for analytic work.

TREATMENT

In this case we can observe some of the delicate and subtle aspects of working with the borderline/narcissistic couple. Initially, borderlines want quick-fix answers because they cannot tolerate frustration due to their impaired judgment faculties and their lack of impulse control. With the borderline patient, a psychic structure emerges that is closer to perversion than has often been considered. Borderlines fear expressing their real needs; they dread that they will be ridiculed, betrayed, or rejected. While they seek out relatedness, they are often unable to make use of it, since their original trauma in many cases severely impaired their capacity for healthy object relations. Here we digress a bit and go back to psychoanalytic theory. Therapists familiar with self psychology and object relations recognize that too much empathy for the borderline may be misinterpreted as a collusion with the pathology. As mentioned earlier, borderlines, in particular, need a hard object to stand up against (Lachkar 1992). In general, the borderline can make better use of the therapist as container or hard object than can the narcissist. On the surface, the borderline may appear resentful, angry, attacked, but in the long run will feel soothed and relieved to know that the therapist is caring enough to enter his inner world. Children who have been emotionally abused need a parent who can stand up for them. In some instances when this is not the case, the unavailability becomes more destructive than the abuse itself. Many of us spend endless hours listening to our patients repeat the same injuries again and again because they have a desperate need to have someone bear witness to their testimony. Children who missed the validation suffer the most. We are working with volatile feelings and people lacking in impulse control who need therapists who are not afraid to confront the abuse or mistreatment.

The same type of confrontation would be experienced by the narcissist as a narcissistic injury. The narcissist will withdraw with narcissistic rage or personal injury if she feels her sense of specialness or entitlement is threatened or challenged too early. Instead, she will respond more to empathic responses, mirroring, and interpretation.

Clinicians must consider the emotional internal space in which abusers and victims live. The borderline exists in the depths of despair, his persistent anticipatory anxieties threatening to catapult him into an endless emotional black hole. The narcissist moves within an omnipotent world, filled with fantasies of restoration to her previous position of being adored. Her hopes have long since been dashed, replaced by excessive entitlement fantasies.

As we saw in the previous chapter, the most difficult task facing the therapist is to know when and how to take on the narcissist's omnipotence. This omnipotence will begin to diminish as the narcissist realizes that life is enhanced by attending to one's true needs and allowing for imperfection. For the borderline, the crucial task is to help the patient comprehend how he either splits off or projects his needs and shame into the other. Once he understands that this splitting or projection is at the heart of his impaired judgment and inner chaos, even of his sudden outbursts, he will be able to start accepting ambiguity and considering that his needs can be met in ways that do not involve the abandonment of himself or the destruction of the other.

One of the purposes of the therapeutic alliance is to help the borderline acquire these skills. But borderline abusers, particularly those with paranoid features, may mistrust our every motive. They are a challenge to therapists because they provoke in the countertransference various counteraggressive reactions, and also at times the therapist's wish to offer quick-fix solutions. When this occurs, the therapist must be willing to use her countertransference to understand the borderline's experience with others and to communicate this understanding to her patient.

In conjoint therapy, the notion of dual projective identification, the "dance," offers a compelling vision of the couple's interactions as they mutually project and identify with the projections of each other. Partners in these troubled adult relationships are in complicity with one another, their dance mutually choreographed. From this perspective, it becomes clear that each is a victim and each participates in the abuse due to his or her own split-off or projected needs. In learning that their original true self needs are normal and appropriate, they can allow space for them within their current relationship.

As the therapy progresses through its various phases (see Chapter 8), each partner begins to face not only his or her external abusers, but the internal abusers as well. Conjoint therapy is an intense experience for all three of the participants, couple and therapist, setting off deep emotions regarding false and true self needs and the communications of these needs. Although the personality styles and defenses of each partner are well-entrenched, with each session the window of opportunity opens a bit more, and the possibility for a new experience increases.

ᴥ 5 ᴥ

The Passive-Aggressive Abuser

There we were in the south of France. It was our fifteenth wedding anniversary. I finally got my husband to take me away on a lovely trip when suddenly I found out he hadn't made any reservations. All the rooms and hotels were *complete* [French for occupied]. All I heard was the word *complete, complete, complete.* When I asked why he didn't make the reservations, he offered his usual barrage of excuses: "I kept calling, and all I got was a busy signal. I wasn't feeling well. I had a big mess in the office. My phone wasn't working. The secretary was out ill." Then he expected me to feel sorry for him—which I did.

THE PASSIVE-AGGRESSOR

Although the passive-aggressive disorder has been replaced with negativistic personality disorder in the current *DSM-IV*, I still find that it has applicability for couple therapy. I therefore take the liberty to extend its usage to the treatment of emotional abuse. Of all the personality disorders described here, this one has the most difficulty in interpersonal relations because the passive-aggressive always transforms his relations into a parent–child matrix. The passive-aggressive personality defends against the expectations and demands of others by functioning from a dependent and infantile position, and uses passivity as an unconscious expression of aggression. Passive-aggressiveness is often a product of unresolved sibling rivalry, where avoidance was the main artery for emotional escape. This kind of individual routinely procrastinates, feigns inefficiency, and invariably offers a plethora of excuses as to why various tasks were not accomplished. Passive-aggressives experience others as exerting unrealistic pressure upon them, and defend against commitments by ineptness and forgetfulness, devaluing the needs of others as well as devaluing the importance of the tasks required of them.

In "Instincts and Their Vicissitudes," Sigmund Freud (1915) emphasizes that activity is a defining quality of the instincts: "Every instinct is a piece of activity; if we speak of passive instincts, we can only mean instincts whose aim is passive" (pp. 214–215). Even though the borderline cannot make good use of selfobjects, at least he has the desire to bond. As we shall see in the following chapter, the obsessive-compulsive actively carries out his need for order and structure. But with the passive-aggressive personality, activity of the instincts is replaced by the aim of dependency.

What are the origins of the passive-aggressive disorder and its enactments? The primary emotional environment in the early life of the passive-aggressive shows a marked prohibition against the direct expression of affect, particularly anger or hostility. Often, these children were made to conform to impossible standards and were not encouraged or even allowed to express emotions. When they did, they were severely criticized or castigated.

THE PASSIVE-AGGRESSIVE ABUSER

The passive-aggressive abuser has not received much attention, for s/he is not an obvious abuser, but a subtle one. Unlike the borderline, the passive-aggressive abuser is an unconscious bully. "Who me? I didn't do that!" The patient with borderline organization will initially comply only to lash out later, or will spend inordinate amounts of time and energy seeking vengeance on the person who was felt to have abandoned or betrayed him. The narcissist, too, is more direct in openly expressing his disdain and lack of interest. At least with the narcissist, there is some level of superego organization in the grandiose self so that there is a sense of responsibility. By contrast, the passive-aggressive's stories are filled with a barrage of mishaps resulting in the inability to fulfill expectations of self and other. The passive-aggressive feels persecuted by the needs of others. Aggression is an essential component of his behavior. Unable to express his feelings openly and honestly he acts out by burdening his partner with parental responsibilities. He is one of the most difficult to treat because he is highly manipulative and uses maneuvers such as procrastination, obstinacy, recalcitrance, forgetfulness, dawdling, and stubbornness. All these enactments are unconsciously designed to project rage into the object in order to rid his psyche of aggression. At his core, there is the desire to be at-one in harmony and symbiosis in the universe without any disturbance.

THE PASSIVE AGGRESSIVE'S DEFENSES

Disconnected from feelings of shame or guilt, passive-aggressive abusers resort to defenses of splitting, projective identification, and avoidance in order to coerce others to perform functions for them. They operate at the most primitive level within the paranoid-schizoid position. Dominated as they are by their lack of autonomous ego and superego functioning, they use others as part-objects and seek out objects who will allow them to maintain their dependency patterns. The passive-aggressive will use every opportunity to shift the relationship into the mother–child dyad, especially with a responsible maternal figure. In defending against the pressures of fulfilling commitments, passive-aggressives employ others to do their work for them. They are not goal-oriented, are non-assertive, and are almost psychotic in their persistent unconscious demands on others.

Not uncommonly, they show no real incentive to change in treatment, and may respond with aggression, bewilderment, or pseudoconformity to the therapist much as they respond in their intimate relationships. They will cajole and manipulate, attempting to maneuver the therapist into a similar transferential dyadic relationship, even at the cost of insight and awareness (Wolberg 1977).

THE HIGH-FUNCTIONING PARTNERS OF PASSIVE-AGGRESSIVE ABUSERS

The women who are drawn to and stay with passive-aggressive partners are frequently masochistic. These women strive for positions of authority by being well educated and diligent, but also identify with their mothers in the notion that all men are inherently helpless. They are the caretakers, the women who are self-sacrificing yet perfectionistic. These women were often the "little adults," those who took care of siblings or who were mothers to their own mothers. It is very easy for these women to fall into the parent–child relationship that passive-aggressive men induce. They identify with the parent, becoming "mommy" as their mate becomes baby brother or inept child instead of an equal and mutual partner.

These high-functioning but masochistic women learned to respond to emotional "carrots" from parents who dangled these goodies in front of them while inevitably breaking their implied promises. Such parents provided the function of both the enticing and the disappointing object. Additionally, they mocked the child's normal dependency needs, making the child feel useless, sinful, or shameful unless she fulfilled certain functions or roles for the parents. Understanding these insidious interplays between the parents' tantalizations and the child's strivings allows us to see how adult masochistic women get attached to passive-aggressive men, only to be disappointed repeatedly when they depend on them. We also can comprehend how these high-functioning women are so capable in their jobs, and yet so unfulfilled at home. To give up the lure that the "carrot" holds would mean to be plunged into unremitting isolation and grief.

THE DANCE

In the dance between the passive-aggressive abuser and his high-functioning, masochistic partner, a complex array of enactments are set in motion. The high-functioning woman evokes the possibility for the passive-aggressive that his dependency needs can be met by her competence and caregiving. But the high-functioning woman will be looking to her passive-aggressive partner as the one who promises her the world. When her expectations become another source of impossible demands for him, the passive-aggressive partner withdraws into passivity. As he does so, he becomes the enticing object who disappoints once again, and the high-functioning woman will pursue more desperately the fulfillment of her needs through both her demands and her caregiving functions. This increases the pressure felt by the passive-aggressive who then blames his partner, and ultimately withdraws into psychic isolation to avoid unmanageable conflict and confrontation. And on and on the cycle escalates, ultimately making both partners feel that they are—or at least one of them is—bad and wrong.

CASE ILLUSTRATION: THE FORGETFUL PASSIVE-AGGRESSIVE ABUSER

Lori, a high-functioning borderline personality, is an executive with an international corporation. Every time her passive-aggressive attorney husband, Forrest, is supposed to make an appropriate dinner reservation, he "forgets" or waits until so late that the restaurant of choice is packed and unable to take their reservation. Lori becomes incensed, as Forrest frantically proceeds to search for a restaurant that is open, sometimes driving around for hours before dinner. Finally, they settle for any restaurant able to seat them and their guests. Once again, Lori ends up feeling worthless, disappointed, and abused. She becomes the proprietor of the rage: "If you ever do this again, I will kill you!" she screams. Forrest is relieved; he's paid off his emotional mortgage. Now, he is free to blame her for being so demanding. He withdraws, and the "dance" goes on.

Lori: He always forgets. Is it right for him to forget to buy the food? There I was at a birthday party for our daughter with 25 little kids, and Forrest never showed up with the balloons, the diapers, or the cake. He always does this to me!

Therapist: Perhaps we're better off trying to understand what's beneath the forgetfulness, the lateness, the non-caring attitude [therapist showing a point of view but not dwelling on it].

Forrest: I don't forget, nor do I not care, and I resent you saying that!

Therapist: You sound angry.

Forrest: No, I'm not angry!

Therapist: I was hoping you were angry, because it would be much more up front and far better than forgetting or being continually late.

Forrest: But I don't forget.

Therapist: Actually, that's not quite the case. You have forgotten things here as well.

Forrest: What have I forgotten here?

Therapist: Well, for instance, you've forgotten appointments, payments, or have kept me waiting [opening up transference issues].

Lori: I can't believe you just said that. All my life I've been mistreated, abused, invalidated. No one has ever stood up for me before. My mother always went along with my father, even when he was just plain wrong.

Therapist: I'm glad you felt supported by me. [Turning to Forrest] I would like you, Forrest, to also feel my support.

Forrest: I don't. I feel attacked.

Therapist: You feel when I'm direct with you, I'm attacking you.

Forrest: That's what people have done to me my whole life.

Therapist: Like your big brothers picking on you when you were small, being mean and condescending?

Forrest: Yes.

Therapist: I did not intend to pick on you, though I can see how it might feel that way to you. In fact, I really meant to be helpful, because I feel you would relate better with your wife and would have a better marriage if you could be more direct with her, even if that means getting angry.

Forrest: I want to, but when I'm direct she just puts me down.

Lori: Actually, I would appreciate you being more direct with me.

Therapist: [to Lori] Why haven't you encouraged this, then?

Lori: Because I knew it wouldn't make any difference. He's just like my father.

Therapist: Ah, this is very useful! I can see now how you both lose your boundaries. Lori, Forrest becomes the father who didn't listen to your needs or the helpless baby brother you had to take care of. Forrest, Lori becomes the sadistic, dangerous, tormenting sibling who's out to get you. Instead of each of you seeing the other as the spouse whom you love and who presumably loves you in return, you are each experiencing the other as the one who hurt or deprived you in your early lives.

Lori: That's how it's been my whole life. My mother always took advantage of me. I was the caretaker for her and, as the eldest child, she put me in charge of my baby brother. My parents always promised that after I did my chores, they would do things with me, but they never did.

Forrest: [to Therapist] You know, even though I don't always like the things you say to me, I must admit I really enjoy your directness. It's amazing to me that when you're direct, something gets done.

Therapist: That's precisely the point. If I were passive here, nothing would get accomplished. I would just be fusing or colluding with Lori's early experience, or going along with and encouraging yours, Forrest. And that's what happens between the two of you.

[To Forrest] As you agree to demands that feel

overwhelming to you, you don't keep them. Instead, you expect Lori to be the executive at home, like she is at work, placing her in the same position she was in as a child. Lori then feels you have enticed her with your false promises and disappointed her, just as her parents did. When you attack her, you force her to re-engage with her high-functioning self, abandoning her own needs.

[To Lori] As you place demands on Forrest with greater and greater intensity, you become the parent who has impossible expectations of him. As he feels more and more overwhelmed, he withdraws into passivity. When he disappoints you, you attack him and become his dangerous big brothers, and he retreats further or retaliates. Neither of you can then hold onto the relationship you have as two adults who love one another, in a mutually caring relationship.

Forrest: (laughing) I forget that!

Lori: So do I!

DISCUSSION

Understanding the notion of dual projective identification is extremely helpful. In this case, the dance between a high-functioning but masochistic woman and her passive-aggressive husband can help us as clinicians in learning to deal with subtle forms of emotional abuse.

Obviously, Forrest is not going to go to jail for his passivity or his failure to be on time, make reservations, or remember to buy balloons and diapers. Even his verbal attacks against Lori are not enough to create legal problems for him. Nobody is going to sue Lori for making demands or for her retaliation when she is disappointed. Still, each of these individuals feels in the painful interactions with one another a replication of emotional abuse.

What makes Forrest not only passive-aggressive but an abuser as well? Forrest clearly has narcissistic and borderline features, for he is easily susceptible to narcissistic injury and fusional/collusional states leading to loss of self and identity confusion. He also readily responds to injury with the borderline's all too familiar attacks on the other. If Forrest were more predominantly narcissistic, he would, ironically, have a stronger sense of self. If he were more predominantly borderline, he would make greater efforts to please Lori in order to satisfy his dependency needs. Instead, he carries as his primary organizing principle many inherent pathogenic characteristics and states of the passive aggressive: he experiences expectations as punitive and overwhelming demands, and he uses passivity to search out psychic safety. When his retreat from perceived danger does not offer the safety he seeks, he retaliates as a passive bully, disclaiming, undermining, and thrusting Lori into the same untenable position she was in with her parents. He cannot be honest with her; instead, he splits off his own needs, or projects into her the rage he was not allowed to express to his parents.

This relationship is in dire need of boundaries, not a quick fix. Each partner is going to need the therapist to be clear, honest, and active. Lori needs the therapist to support her in some of her expectations, to make clear when her needs are reasonable. She can make use of interpretations, and she will shift more easily out of her masochistic enactments than her spouse will shift out of his passivity. In calling attention to Forrest's failure to comply with the boundaries of the treatment, just as he fails in meeting Lori's expectations, the therapist risks the possible collapse of the treatment with Forrest. Due to the sadism of Forrest's older brothers, the therapist's intervention will be felt as an attack. A possible aid in this dilemma would be to prepare Forrest ahead of time for interpretations that may be felt as emotionally taxing. Consider the following:

> Forrest, there will be times in this treatment when certain issues will be called to your attention, and you may experience these interpretations as an attack. If this occurs, I would like you to express these feelings and talk about your desire to retreat. You may talk about whatever emotional experience you are having here in safety, but you will only discover this if you give yourself the opportunity to express what you're feeling, so that we can work on it.

While it is unlikely that Forrest will believe in this proposed safety, such preparation provides a good touchstone for the therapy when the patient feels in psychic danger. The therapist then can remind the patient of their earlier conversation and say: "This is one of those times I mentioned that might feel dangerous for you, and I want to encourage you to take the risk in discussing what you're feeling so that you may discover that there is psychic safety for you here."

At the end of the session presented in this case, there seemed to be more integration in both Lori and Forrest, but we must not be deluded into thinking that their primitive dance will not repeat itself. Of course it will.

In conjoint therapy, the therapist must be able to advocate for the rightful needs of each partner, as well as point out why those needs repeatedly are unmet within the patients' intimate relationship. The therapist must have a clear and open mind, create a safe and flexible environment, and be firm enough to avoid providing special favors (waiting for payment, allowing consistent lateness for appointments or forgetfulness).

TREATMENT

The passive-aggressive is a closet abuser and a difficult patient with whom to make progress. And this is because the very expectation of progress can be experienced by the passive-aggressive as another demand upon him. He resents interpretations, regarding them as unfair criticisms. Usually, he is antagonistic to any implication that there may be a defect in him. He may respond with a panoply of reactions: bewilderment, pseudoconformity, and withdrawal.

In treatment, the hope for progress often rests far more with the masochistic partner of the passive-aggressive. Once she realizes how she is drawn repeatedly into pursuing the dangling "carrot," she can attempt to curtail her overt expectations. Further, as she understands that much of the rage she experiences in the face of the passive-aggressive's enactments is rage projected into her by the passive-aggressive, she is able to find other ways of responding to her disappointment. Progress for the victim will depend upon how much she continues to identify with the passive-aggressive's projections, and, more significantly, if she is able to relinquish the hope that the promises of long ago will be fulfilled today.

One can see that with the passive-aggressive abuser a "quick-fix" approach without an in-depth understanding of both the disorder and the dynamics involved might mislead the therapist into thinking the patient has absorbed insight and understanding. The therapist must remain alert to the passive-aggressive's ploys, which constantly seek to maintain the infantile replication of the parent–child dyad.

Treatment of the passive-aggressive abuser and the masochistic, high-functioning woman consists of encouraging both partners to become more open to the experience of their own needs and the needs of the other, and to be expressive of their psychic experience. For this openness and interaction to occur, the therapist must be actively engaged in the triadic interchange (couple transference). To do so the therapist must have a point of view. While it is still popular today among many classical theorists to appear void of judgment and to function as a "blank screen," to do so with the passive-aggressive and masochistic couple in conjoint therapy is to collude with the defeatist part of each partner and the couple's dual projective identification.

How far can we go in conjoint treatment with the passive-aggressive abuser and the high-functioning, masochistic woman? Only as far as the therapist and each member of the couple are willing to go. Many clinicians hold that the therapeutic task is to offer immediate relief from conflict (Lachkar 1992). The "cure," however, does not have a curative effect if it does not address the unconscious wishes or desires of the patients or the developmental issues involved. If couples want such immediate relief, they need to understand that it was just the desire for the "quick fix" that got them into the difficulty in the first place. One paid an extraordinary price for the quick fix in the original harmful experiences, just as one does in replicating that wish in the couple's current relationship and in the therapy. We must educate our patients that the focus is not the relationship, but each partner's developmental issues. It is impossible to experience a "real relationship" when there is so much rage, shame and blame, idealization, withdrawal, avoidance, and denial in the enactments.

In treating the passive-aggressive abuser, it is essential to recognize that hostility in both the transference and the countertransference is inevitable. The demands of dependent patients are so intense that it is impossible not to fail the patient at some point. However, when such therapeutic failures are used as opportunities for understanding the original trauma, the passive-aggressive can begin to experience himself and others as people with legitimate needs. The goal of the therapy is to promote an environment in which both partners can come to understand the failures that occurred in their early years and to accept responsibility for their own needs within current interactions.

⸺ 6 ⸻

The Obsessive-Compulsive Abuser

He makes me feel crazy. One minute he's yelling about how much money I've spent on a new, expensive ensemble, and the next he's telling me about a client's wife who dresses exquisitely, wears expensive jewelry, and drives a new model Mercedes-Benz. How come it's all right for her to have nice things, but not for me? Why does he do this to me? Why does he put me down for wanting them, saying that I'm too demanding and there is no way of pleasing me?

THE OBSESSIVE-COMPULSIVE

The obsessive-compulsive personality clusters with many other personality disorders, so it may be difficult to determine what is and what is not within the obsessive-compulsive range.[1] Commonly, in obsessional neurosis,

---

1. The obsessive-compulsive personality (OCPDA) must be distinguished from the Obsessive-Compulsive Disorder (OCD). The OCD is ego dystonic, in need of behavioral and perhaps pharmacological treatment, and has symptoms that are disabling

the obsessive-compulsive manifests intrapsychic conflict in two ways. Internally, obsessional thinking results in repetitive thought patterns, endless ruminations, and paralyzing doubt. Externally, obsessional thinking patterns take the form of uncontrollable compulsive behaviors.

Similar to the borderline, the obsessive-compulsive confuses needs and feelings with something dangerous and persecutory. The obsessive-compulsive is anal retentive, withholding, and will turn to the use of money, time, drugs, order, relationships, and duty in addictive ways to ward off the internal "messy" parts of himself.

Just as we have seen with the passive-aggressive abuser, this disorder develops out of the individual's need for psychic safety. At the base of this disorder is often the lack of secure attachment to the parental figure early in life. Combined with this absence of attachment was the demand for performance from the parents, making the child's eventual individuation a source of intense conflict, usually resulting in failure.

We see in obsessive-compulsive patients the tendency to mull over and over the minute details of a situation or relationship, and thereby lose the larger

---

and immobilizing for the patient. Patients with OCD are often severe hoarders, pathological pack rats, or counter checkers. Since these patients are in need of special treatment, this book does not address the OCD disorder.

context of their encounters. To manage affective experiences, obsessive-compulsives compartmentalize feelings. Therefore, they are restricted in their ability to express emotions or develop intimate involvements. Their compulsion to be orderly and clean emanates from their intolerance of the chaos of their early lives and their inability to deal with such chaos. Projecting their confusion and dependence into others provides the only avenue for psychic safety, justifying their harsh withholding of time, energy, attention, money, or gifts.

The greater the level of disturbance, the more the obsessive-compulsive's enactments become out of control. For the severe obsessive-compulsive, desires, needs, dependency, and emotional vulnerability are equivalent to feces and filth. In spite of the obsessive-compulsive's deep needs to be attached and dependent, he will denounce such needs either by attacking the other or by being quick to avoid intimate contacts. If he is able to sustain any kind of relationship with others, his projections into them are ferocious and his demands insatiable.

Paradoxically, despite his projections of his "badness"—his "dirt"—the obsessive-compulsive remains attached to this same dirt. Many obsessive-compulsives become pack rats, unable to discard worn-out clothing, old newspapers, magazines, or even string and wire. They have remained fused to mother's body in the ongoing attempt to attach; unwittingly, they are unable to detach from those objects that represent the promise of the mother's body. The pack rat lives inside a dark, tight, anal world, packed with clutter that offers a nostalgic hope for an attachment that will never occur.

THE OBSESSIVE-COMPULSIVE ABUSER

The obsessive-compulsive abuser is an individual who spends considerable psychic energy projecting his unacceptable needs into the object in the attempt to evacuate what he believes are the bad parts of himself, and then attacking the object for that badness. The superego of obsessive-compulsive abusers has aspects of hatred and sadism. These proclivities are especially noticeable in their need to control, dominate, and even humiliate (Kernberg 1992). In order to retain the good "dutiful" parts of the self, obsessive-compulsive abusers will become preoccupied with small, tedious tasks, insist upon strict rules, or become absorbed with making lists and redoing schedules. They devote themselves excessively to work and perfection, even to the point of dismissing leisure activities and family and social relations.

Because of their fanatical commitment to work, they are often successful breadwinners and take great pride in being providers. However, their authoritarianism and self-righteousness make others feel helpless. The obsessive-compulsive's exaggerated sense of self-worth is measured in terms of what he can do rather than who he is. Both borderlines and obsessive-compulsives confuse how things feel with how things are.

The attitude of the obsessive-compulsive abuser is: "I'm the man of the house and don't you forget it!" He pays a heavy emotional price for the sacrifice of his own inner needs and feelings in his attempts at finding psychic safety and a sense of self-worth. So do those around him. Obsessive-compulsives desire contact and intimacy but cannot understand how their behaviors impede the process because they are so dutifully "correct." They do not invite emotions and are restricted in their ability to express them or to offer time, money, praise, and gifts. Emotional abuse occurs because of the bind in which the obsessive-compulsive finds himself: the internal threat of his dependency needs and the search for a psychic safety he cannot obtain except through the projection of those archaic needs into his partner.

THE HIGH-FUNCTIONING PARTNERS OF OBSESSIVE-COMPULSIVE ABUSERS

The obsessive-compulsive abuser is most inclined to join up with a woman who is of a hysterical nature (Sperry and Maniaci 1997). The obsessive-compulsive, along with the narcissist and the schizoid, evokes intense feelings of envy and rivalry. These are men who "need their space," and disparage their partners' healthy dependency needs.

The notion of hysterical disease was conceptualized as far back as Hippocrates, and the evolution in the understanding of this neurosis has followed the developmental line of the history of medicine itself. Today, two primary forms of hysteria neurosis that Breuer and Freud (1893–1895) delineated are still considered the valid basis for the comprehension of hysteria: (1) conversion hysteria, in which psychic conflict within the individual is expressed in a variety of somatic symptoms, and (2) anxiety hysteria, in which anxiety is attached to an external object, as in a phobia. It is not easy to pinpoint hysterical symptoms. Often, the patient is unaware of a traumatic experience and is unable to connect to a precipitating event.

Often, in our society, as an individual seeks a partner, s/he will look for someone who will provide an aspect missing from him- or herself. For the obsessive-compulsive, who seeks psychic safety in the rejection of his own needs, the hysteric woman appears to offer the warmth, generosity, and gregariousness for which he yearns. While these qualities may indeed be present, the obsessive-compulsive will soon learn that his partner can also be impulsive, explosive, and exhibitionistic. The hysteric woman, especially one who is high-functioning professionally, will seek out to a mate who appears orderly, conservative, and methodical as a balance for her own inner chaos and reactivity, only to discover the controlling, manipulative, and distancing aspects of the obsessive-compulsive's personality.

Hysteric women often carry substantial unconscious guilt through their enmeshment with an internally severe and prohibitive mother. Sexuality arouses guilt, rekindling unconscious memories of the reprisals they experienced as children when their sexual nature was developing. Many hysterics were molested in childhood or abused in a variety of ways. Often they responded to their early traumas by becoming extremely dependent, needing others to assume responsibility for them. Still other hysterics become phobically attached to acting out exhibitionist tendencies. The hysteric has poor impulse control as the result of experiencing overwhelming affect, and is inclined to act out in ways that she later deeply regrets. For the hysteric, at first glance the obsessive-compulsive offers stability and security, and to him she offers aliveness and spontaneity.

THE DANCE

When the obsessive-compulsive and the hysteric come together in intimate relationships, they play out familiar scenarios. The obsessive-compulsive male is drawn to the hysteric woman because she exhibits an emotional presence he has long ago abandoned. Yet, within a short time this very emotionality becomes threatening to the obsessive-compulsive's equilibrium. For him, his partner's feminine charms now become clinging behaviors, her warmth becomes sweltering, her sexual evocativeness and exhibitionism become disgusting. When the obsessive-compulsive responds by becoming controlling and excessively methodical, the hysteric's demands only increase. In one such scenario, we can see a stereotypical enactment between two partners: the obsessive-compulsive husband buys material objects for his wife as his only available expression of love and commitment, while accusing her of being an impulsive shopper and someone who should not need or is not deserving of his gifts. The attacked wife cannot feel emotionally satisfied by the material objects and becomes only more demanding as her internal needs go unmet. She is then demeaned as hysterical by a husband in full psychic retreat.

For the hysteric, the stability and reassurance that the obsessive-compulsive's orderly presence originally provided becomes but another repudiation of who she is and what she needs, leaving her re-traumatized in her current partnership. As Sperry and Maniaci (1997) put it, the hysteric/obsessive-compulsive couple is the "love sick" wife and the "cold sick" husband. The structure the hysteric sought as comforting and stabilizing is now constricting. The obsessive-compulsive's appearance of self-containment reveals itself to be inhibition, and his hard work and provision of material security seems a cold comfort. Instead of a partner upon whom she can lean and with whom she can find fulfillment of her dependency needs, she finds herself trapped with a controlling and judgmental mate—the replication of her internalized severe and prohibiting parent.

The abuse that the obsessive-compulsive and hysteric experience as they come together in unison is the search for missing aspects of themselves. The attack upon and rejection of their true selves and their early, normal, and reasonable needs is a replication of their original injuries. In their flight from the painful absence of fulfillment of those needs, they find in each other a partner who appears to offer relief but who, in fact, resimulates the detached or prohibitive parent with whom there can be no psychic safety.

CASE ILLUSTRATION:
THE WORKAHOLIC ABUSER

Alan contacted me after reading about a couple in my book on narcissistic and borderline couples—a pair who reminded him of his own dilemma. "I believe my wife is the borderline, and I am the narcissist," he said.

When he and his wife and I met for the initial conjoint session, I noticed his impeccable grooming. He exuded elegance in every detail of his dress, with his monogrammed shirt, his perfectly knotted necktie, his gold cuff links, and the folded handkerchief in his breast pocket. He initially appeared to be very aware both of himself and others, communicating a precise sense of his own dynamics. He explained that he was an attorney with a tendency to work too much. His wife, Janet, an attractive woman who worked as an editor of a fashion magazine, seemed pleasant enough, yet I sensed in her an impatience. If pushed, she appeared to be someone who could easily explode.

Over the first few conjoint sessions, it became clear that Alan was an obsessive-compulsive and that Janet was a hysteric. Alan revealed himself to be a self-righteous and morally rigid man. He maintained that he did not mean to be critical but felt preoccupied with seeing that things got done the "right way." In their daily life, he refused to help her with the dishes or other household chores, claiming he was far too busy and important, and he continually refused to flush the toilet, even in the guest bathroom. Janet, a self-proclaimed feminist, felt humiliated by his behavior. And as for his bathroom habits, she feared guests would view her as the messy one. At one early session, some of the struggles they experienced with one another became evident.

Alan: I do like to work. As a matter of fact, I'm working on a new software program that will allow attorneys all over the nation to tap into my database. [Alan explained both his program and database in elaborate detail, while Janet began to squirm and roll her eyes, before finally looking at me in desperation as if pleading with me to rescue her from the onslaught of her husband's discourse. Finally, she interrupted.]

Janet: What do you mean you like to work? You're a workaholic! [To the therapist] With Alan, everything has to be perfect. He contends that I do not wash the kitchen utensils. When we have dinner, he complains about the food.

Alan: I always try to tell Janet that she needs to be neater around the house, to be more organized, and if only she would listen to me, she could run a better household.

Janet: He wants constant attention, all my time, and when I can't give him those things because of my work, he makes me feel so guilty. Once he got so enraged with me he took the trash bag and threw it at me. Even worse are his expectations that I ought to be as perfect as he thinks he is, and his continual put-downs when I'm not.

Therapist: I think what you are referring to as perfection is the expression of your husband's needs. Maybe he experiences those needs as being messy.

Janet: But I wouldn't mind if he were too needy; instead, he's too controlling. Everything has to be done his way, and when it's not, he becomes like a baby. He's disgusting. How would you like your husband to leave his feces unflushed in the toilet? "Give me, do me, listen to me, watch me"—that's what he says all the time, one way or another. I can't stand it! He either always has to be right or else he becomes demanding like a needy baby. It's such a turn-off!

Therapist: I can understand how you feel, but we're here to try and understand how being needy might feel like an unflushed toilet. What's wrong with being needy?

Janet: I find it disgusting. It's like opening up a can of worms. I don't want to deal with all that. I don't need anything. I'm perfectly happy being an independent woman.

Therapist: So needs are disgusting for you, yours and Alan's? [Needs are felt by each partner as hostile internal persecutors.] Is it possible that needs can be seen as worthy of respect, that they don't have to be viewed as a can of worms or as garbage?

Janet: That's true, but he doesn't understand that. At work, I'm in control. Men in my firm treat me with respect. I deal with many advertising and business people every day, but when I come home I feel abused and am treated like nothing. I don't understand how I can be these two different people. I feel so stupid and ashamed. None of my friends can possibly understand how tortured I feel with Alan.

Therapist: You're saying you feel emotionally abused?

Alan: What do you mean, emotionally abused? Are you calling me an abuser?

Therapist: I am trying to reflect your wife's feelings and I do believe this is how Janet experiences you. But I am also trying to understand the particular state of mind you get into, Alan, when you feel things may not be perfect or when you don't feel in control. This seems to make you anxious, causing you to react in a way you may not want to. There are other ways to respond, but I think you're afraid you will lose control and become too dependent, too needy. You may even feel stupid for having normal and healthy needs.

Alan: [Unable to take in the therapist's words] You bet it makes me feel anxious, because I *am* perfect. I have to be perfect and have had to be perfect my whole life. Okay, then what should I do? Should we stay together or get a divorce?

Therapist: Do you want me to respond like your database? With a quick answer? Wouldn't that be another way your needs would be forfeited, this time by me? Instead, let's use your computer as a metaphor. Your needs are not viruses or bugs, invading and then ruining you, but an important part of your emotional life. Needs are an essential part of our internal software programs, without which we couldn't run our hard drives.

Alan: I never thought of it that way before.

Therapist: I think it's easier for you to focus on doing rather than feeling. You think that to be vulnerable and dependent or to tolerate a feeling of smallness in yourself or Janet is tantamount to garbage, in other words, being less than perfect. If you were to allow yourself to be needy, to be vulnerable, I believe there would be a little boy inside who feels very frightened and intimidated, especially when not in control.

Janet: He always has to be in control. If food touches my hands, he won't eat the food. I happen to be a very clean and meticulous woman, but he slams the door and screams out loud that he'd rather be dead than eat in this filth, dirt, and slop. Then I start to cry and scream. I hate his needs and his being after me all the time. Later, when I calm down, I think to myself, I am a professional woman. Everyone else treats me like a queen, except for Alan who treats me as if I'm garbage.

Therapist: You both have to take responsibility for the behaviors you express. Alan, you have no right to throw a bag of garbage at Janet, or to control her, or to accuse her of things that are not true. This is abusive behavior. Janet, you need to take responsibility for some of your "garbage throwing." Alan's needs for attention and time with you may not always be excessive. You make him feel bad for being dependent or too needy. These are some of the issues we can work on together, and though we have to stop for today, we'll continue next session.

DISCUSSION

Over many months, both Janet and Alan revealed far deeper conflicts. As an adult, Alan was still unable to separate internally from an intrusive and messy mother. He masturbated compulsively and felt great shame at this behavior. He felt that he could never get anything clean enough and hid his own excessive and ritualistic behaviors regarding cleanliness and order. In fantasy, Alan believed that his masturbatory hands would infect and destroy everything.

Janet, who was molested as a child, experienced Alan's compulsivity and excessive need for cleanliness as his way of escaping injured feelings and vulnerabilities, which he perceived as tantamount to dirt. As in many intimate relations, Alan's need to control Janet stirred up fantasies of getting rescued, fantasies she found intolerable in her push for independence. Her own desperate needs to be seen and cared for made her feel so wrong and bad that they threw her into internal states of helplessness. She would then become hysterical, vacillating from molested, terrorized child to a woman appalled at her own behavior.

Eventually, we were able to understand how each partner identified with the projections of the other, feeling attacked and persecuted. Our major task for the first months of the therapy was to name the emotional abuse when it did occur, and to point out to both partners that even though there may be an external abuser, a "garbage thrower," there is also the taking in and participating with the abuse via the process of dual projective identification.

TREATMENT

"Tell us what to do! Should we stay together or get a divorce?" Patients in marital treatment are always insisting that therapists tell them what to do. Their need for relief from the persecution they feel is so intense that almost any solution offered would be embraced. The therapist will have significant countertransference issues to deal with, especially as s/he is pulled into the desire to provide the relief the patients are seeking. Instead, the therapeutic task must be the gradual weaning away from what the couple is "doing" to their "being." When patients are in the blaming/attacking phase, when there is such intense rage, avoidance, idealization, denial, or persecutory anxiety present in the therapy between partners and/or enacted with the therapist, it is difficult for each member of the triad to think about the affect being expressed. It is the therapist's challenge to be able to contain the patients' early experience and to help both partners understand how that experience is being replicated in their intimate exchange.

Bion (1970) describes three kinds of dependency relationships: commensural, symbiotic, and parasitic.

Janet and Alan's mutual dependency needs were of a parasitic nature. Janet believed that having needs was disgusting and dangerous: to need meant being "ugly, babyish," and (in her experience) molested. Alan had insufficient links to his dependency needs, even to the point that he could provoke and then deny how his messiness (the unflushed toilet) could be distasteful to his wife. His spurning of his wife for her supposed messiness created a perverse relationship. It became important to explore further each partner's envious and destructive side, which made him or her turn away from the marital bond toward the "mess." Important in this exploration was coming to understand how Alan and Janet each used external relationships and their transferences with the therapist to perceive even their healthy needs as "the mess."

The greatest challenge in conjoint therapy, especially when the partners involved have different neuroses, is to address the issues and needs of each patient. Because of the difficulties inherent in this task, it can be helpful for each partner to be seen in individual therapy as well as in conjoint treatment.

«© 7 ©»

The Schizoid Abuser

We were in bed, about to make love; suddenly Calvin
jumped up, threw on his clothes and left, saying he
had work to do, insisting it couldn't wait. I tried to
sleep, but tossed and turned. I called again and again,
but he never answered. I stayed up all night, reliving
the experience, asking myself, Why? Why?

THE SCHIZOID

For the schizoid, engulfment, entrapment, and suffocation fantasies permeate the psyche. Intimate relationships are virtually untenable for the schizoid; a close
relationship invites the danger of profound vulnerability
and of being overwhelmed by a sea of emotions. In his
object relations, the schizoid offers minimal involvement, yet finds himself drawn to women who resemble
the smothering maternal object. Untouched by approval
or criticism, he invariably chooses solitary activities,
apparently not needing external stimulation, passion,
gratification, or validation. According to the *DSM-IV*
(1994), the criteria for the schizoid personality are deter-

mined by a life-long indifference to social and interpersonal relations. Such apparent indifference results from a history of maladaptive patterns within the schizoid's relationships, leading to severe impairments in his social functioning.

The schizoid's anxieties about attachment generally originate in one of two ways: either a fragile bond with the parents was broken or the parents were intrusive. In the theater of the child's mind, this intrusiveness was felt to castrate him or to gobble him up. In order to survive the rupture or to shield himself against impingement, the schizoid developed the defense of detachment. The eventual result of this detachment is a flattening of his affective states. He exhibits an emotional coldness that is like affect amnesia.

The schizoid was first conceptualized by Fairbairn (1940) in his *Schizoid Factors in the Personality* as one who had too much representation of the mother/primary object in the inner world. The schizoid differs in profound ways from the narcissist: the narcissist must rid the world of the other in order to substitute a psychic twin to serve as a mirror for himself, feeling overwhelmed by the many internal representations of the primary other. Thus, for the schizoid, to form attachments means to be obliterated.

The schizoid does not appear to suffer from either the loss of emotional life or the need for specialness that haunts the narcissist; the schizoid is far more contained and self-sufficient. Unlike the obsessive-compulsive, who invites emotions but doesn't know how to connect with others, the schizoid lacks the desire for connection at all. Neither does he share the same moral integrity of the obsessive-compulsive, and so he does not feel diminished if he is not the provider. Because the schizoid avoids relationships, he will usually feel duped, pressured, or manipulated into them when he does become involved. Issues of psychic safety are always at the forefront (Manfield 1992): "Whereas the narcissist's successes are in the service of his grandiose defense, the schizoid's successes are in the service of his distance defense" (p. 26).

THE SCHIZOID ABUSER

The central feature of the schizoid abuser is his lack of affect, combined with an almost cruel insensitivity to the needs of others. What is unique about this type of abuser is that he never appears to get hurt, to experience pain, or to feel insulted by accusations concerning his cruelty. In fact, he may even distort an insult by turning it into a compliment: "Yes, that's me, I'm a sonofabitch all right!" Because of the schizoid's insensitivity to the needs and reactions of his partner, he evokes enormous feelings of rage and sadistic responses in her. Unlike the narcissist, who thrives on praise and responds with indignation when he is rebuffed or reproved, the schizoid prefers to be a loner. Neither the schizoid nor the narcissist can tolerate emotional closeness, yet the schizoid is even more threatened when faced with intimacy than is the narcissist. The withdrawal of the schizoid abuser is characteristically distinct from that of the narcissist: the narcissist withdraws when injured; the schizoid withdraws to avoid entrapment. For the most part, the narcissist can engage interpersonally with those who offer a semblance of selfobject promise, whereas the schizoid has no desire for engagement.

A repetitive cycle ensnares the schizoid. He is drawn to an intimate partner because she makes up for a split within himself; soon thereafter, he becomes disenchanted and overwhelmed by the emotionality of his partner, so he pulls away and detaches. The schizoid abuser is like a caged animal who can think only of escape. For him, the anxiety generated by the relationship produces a kind of psychic claustrophobia. His abuse then takes the form of withdrawal and detachment, a self-protective measure to be sure, but one that creates isolation and despair in the partner.

It is not unusual for a schizoid man to bond with a histrionic personality (Sperry and Maniaci 1997), especially through a sexual connection. Histrionic women are characterized by their seductiveness, using their sexuality as a means of bonding with the men they choose. While the schizoid has great difficulty expressing himself emotionally, he is often able to use the sexual playing field for his and his partner's physical pleasure. For the schizoid, the histrionic's charismatic style and provocative behaviors offer aliveness and vivacity, filling in, in fantasy, his missing parts. Unfortunately, as this same vivacity and intensity of emotions make demands upon him, he is soon overwhelmed and thus retreats to the psychic safety of his isolated self.

The histrionic high-functioning woman holds a special allure. Here is a woman, the schizoid believes, who is not like his mother. Her high-functioning abilities awaken in him the illusion that she will be safer for him, that her professional preoccupations mean he will not have to be intimate. Instead, he soon discovers that because of his partner's neediness, she often has profound, and at times unrealistic, expectations of him. Her emotional requirements cannot be contained, and regardless of how high-functioning she is in her work, it is not her high-functioning self that she brings home but a self that is in a state of psychic starvation. She will anticipate, even demand, an intense emotional connection.

THE DANCE

Since the histrionic woman is willing to bear the responsibility for failures in the relationship with the schizoid man, he feels no guilt when he withdraws or acts aloof. The histrionic woman offers an initial sense of relatedness and connectedness to the schizoid, but through her volatile interactions provides the justification he needs to become isolated, thus perpetuating and exacerbating his already existing pathological system of not needing anyone. As the high-functioning histrionic woman finds this lack of intimate life unbearable, the schizoid will posture: "She's the desperate one! I don't need anyone!"

Again, we wonder, why do these individuals stay in such primitive bonds? Why is it that people will stay in painful, conflictual relations, like a dance, a rondo, that goes round and round? In emotionally abusive relationships, love feelings intersect with aggression, recruiting love to the pathway of malignancy rather than to intimacy and bonding. Not uncommonly, high-functioning women have an inclination to cast away their strong, capable parts when they feel they may have the opportunity to get their more archaic needs met. But the very nature of primitive defenses obscures the ability to think, splits off and projects needs and desires into the object, and causes reality to be distorted. As the high-functioning woman finds that her needs continue to go unmet, her defenses lead her to a greater devaluation of her self as she takes more and more responsibility for the shortcomings in the other. Emotionally abused women are easy targets for denigration because they believe it is they who are ultimately responsible for all the failures in the relationship. This denial of the other's role in the abuse leads to an even more pronounced withering of the self.

Through the dance of dual projective identification, we ascertain how one partner projects into the other the different aspects with which each identifies. Through comprehending and identifying these projections, we can then begin to treat the abuse.

The schizoid is not a deliberate abuser. In fact, the detachment that serves as his refuge is not meant as a personal affront to the partner, but is the primary way he finds psychic safety. However, for the histrionic woman, detachment is the worst fate she can tolerate, one that compels her to press forward more intently, demand more forcefully, and behave more extravagantly—all of which simply hastens and intensifies the schizoid's retreat. For the schizoid, withdrawing into work or recreation is not in itself a withdrawal from his histrionic partner, but a withdrawal from the terror provoked by her intrusive demands upon him. The high-functioning histrionic woman believes that if she were different she might reach him. She tells herself that if she were not so needy he would not withdraw. The histrionic's eroticism is very attractive to the schizoid, and makes her feel she can change him. When he recedes into self-imposed seclusion, she feels crazy and bad—once again. Out of the rage engendered in her, she then attacks. He retreats further, accusing her of being "hysterical" and out of control, even crazy, and thus, he abusively confirms her inner fears.

CASE ILLUSTRATION:
THE TOUCH-ME-NOT ABUSER

Jessica was a successful opera singer; her husband, Calvin, a physicist. Calvin immersed himself in theoretical puzzles, sitting for hours at his computer. "When I'm at my computer, I come alive, my mind is a gold mine! A rush comes over me." Although Jessica originally agreed to Calvin's insistence that each of them maintain separate dwellings, so they could "have their own space," it was an arrangement that was making her miserable. She complained that he "hid" in his house and avoided love-making. "It was driving me crazy. All I could think about was when we would make love, but he kept withholding. I knew Calvin was still attracted to me. In fact, whenever he heard me sing *La Boheme*, he looked entranced. Then that awful night. I've never understood what happened."

In the opening vignette of this chapter we saw Jessica, hurt and bewildered at Calvin's sudden departure as they were engaging in love-making. The following excerpts are from the session with Jessica just after the incident (Session 1), and then their first conjoint session.

Session 1

Jessica: (Crying) Wouldn't you be upset if this happened to you?

Therapist: I can understand why you were upset [validating patient's experience]. You felt abandoned, dropped, just as you did when you were a child and you needed something from your parents and they withdrew.

Jessica: So it's not just me. I thought he loved me and wanted to be with me as much as I wanted to be with him.

Therapist: Do you think it's possible you are able to experience more of what you feel than Calvin is of his own emotional life? That perhaps your marriage means different things to each of you?

Jessica: What do you mean, different things? We are married after all. He tells me how beautiful I am and how sensuous.

Therapist: Yes, but that doesn't necessarily mean that Calvin feels the same way you do. You might imagine that he needs to be involved in exactly the same way you do. It's why children idealize their parents: they cannot bear the idea that what they need to get from their parents isn't possible.

Jessica: That's a horrible thought.

Therapist: It feels that way to you. But it also means that your needs were not bad or wrong, but that the people closest to you didn't know how to meet them.

Jessica: I always chose such crummy, unavailable men. I thought Calvin would be different. He's so committed to his work. He seemed to enjoy everything about me [the histrionic's tendency to overendow the relation-ship]. When we decided to get married, I thought he wanted to keep his house because he could work there. I didn't know it was going to become his hiding place. He's as unavailable as all the others.

Therapist: Just as your parents were unavailable to you?

Jessica: I never thought about that before. You mean I get drawn to men who will withdraw from me like my parents did when they accused me of being too sensitive or said I was too demanding? [the histrionic's capacity for introspection].

Therapist: Yes, and then you focus on how to get them back, and the whole scene replays itself.

Jessica: This is so hard.

Therapist: It is very hard work, work you no longer have to do by yourself.

Jessica: But I crave him. I miss the sex, the passion, the excitement. What do I do about that?

Therapist: First, we need to learn more about your craving. What is so enticing about him? What do you think he promises you?

Jessica: He seems to know a lot. Even though he's quiet, he seems deep, thoughtful. I feel like we could have so much, if only he'd let me in. There must be some way I could change that would make it better. I guess my parents were right. I do need too much.

Therapist: Perhaps your needs aren't bad, but you haven't

been helped to know that there are other ways of getting them met.

Jessica: I can't imagine what those would be.

Therapist: Maybe we'll be able to imagine together.

Session 2

Jessica: I managed to get Calvin to come in today. He wouldn't speak to me for days after this incident, but he did say he would come to treatment with me.

Therapist: Hello, nice to see both of you.

Jessica: It was terrible. Calvin withdrew for so long. I kept calling and calling. Finally, I managed to reach him, and we talked. Maybe he was getting horny, I don't know.

Therapist: [observing Calvin gazing around the room, affectless] Calvin, I'm glad you're here. Would you like to tell me what happened for you in this experience with Jessica?

Calvin: There's really nothing to tell. You heard it all.

Therapist: Then shall I talk with Jessica and any time you wish to participate, you'll do so?

Calvin: I'm just here for Jessica.

Jessica: This is the way he is all the time. When I approach him, he withdraws. He says I remind him of his mother, who was very demanding and domineering and who would smother him with either too much affection or too many demands.

Therapist: Knowing that Calvin feels smothered is a very important thing. [Calvin staring at my books, but obviously listening.]

Jessica: Why is that important? I'm not his mother.

Therapist: No, you're not, and your needs are important. But if there is any hope of getting your needs met, it is essential that you understand how your partner responds to them.

Jessica: My needs are normal. So why does Calvin make me feel like a criminal? Why do I become so panicky when he runs away?

Therapist: You become panicky because you feel his withdrawal has something to do with you.

Calvin: It does. When I decided to marry it was because I thought I had found a woman who was vibrant, alive, and whose life was full enough that she wouldn't be clinging to me all the time. I've found in this last year that there's no end to her needs, emotionally or sexually. She'd make love all night, every night, if she had her way. And she gets so upset. I don't have the time or energy for that. I think she'd swallow me whole if she could, and that wouldn't be enough for her. This happens at work with my colleagues at the university, too. We'll be in a meeting and then everyone wants to continue the meeting over lunch. I go back to the computer lab.

Therapist: Do you run from Jessica or go back to the lab because the involvement feels overwhelming to you?

Calvin: It is overwhelming. If she can't understand that, then our relationship is never going to work.

Jessica: You see, he doesn't really love me.

Calvin: I do love you; that's why I'm here. But I can't be with you all the time, give you what you want the minute you want it. Here you are, an opera singer with a career that's bringing you increasing recognition, but when you're with me, you act like a lovesick child.

Jessica: But that's because you're so aloof. It frightens me. I feel you moving farther and farther away from me. I thought we'd get closer and closer after we were married. I never dreamed we'd be living separate lives, as well as living in separate houses.

Calvin: Well, if you can't get in control of yourself, we will be living separate lives.

DISCUSSION

Calvin does not regard his behavior as a problem. Further, he uses communication as a means of avoiding true communication. His interactions are intended to allow him to withdraw and blame, and to cause Jessica, not himself, to bear the primary responsibility for the survival of the relationship. His superior tone and judgmental attitude make it possible for him to suspend personal and affective interaction.

Profound issues of separation-individuation come to

the fore when the schizoid pairs with the histrionic. Unlike the narcissist who is easily injured, very little affects the schizoid. While aloneness is balm to the schizoid's fears of engulfment, it is his withdrawal that reawakens in his histrionic partner a terror of isolation and feelings of depression. The histrionic woman feels that his emotional escapes are contingent upon her qualities as a woman: she is not sensuous enough or bright enough to maintain his interest.

Yet, the histrionic woman has two almost equal sides to her personality: on the one hand, she is highly emotional and dependent; on the other hand, she has remarkable interactive social skills, is highly motivated to excel, and has the ability to be quite astute and reflective. Her splitting off of her internal qualities can be pronounced enough that she loses access to her strengths when she shifts into her more dependent state.

In fact, as she shifts from one affective state to another, the previous one often feels unreal and untrue to her. When she is strong and vibrant, she may look back on feeling dependent with bewilderment; when she is feeling needy, her strength and vivacity may seem a facade. When she is not inundated by her own swell of emotions, she exhibits a high level of thinking and a capacity to understand complex human patterns. However, when her schizoid partner withdraws and thus abandons her, her strength ebbs and her reasoning and thinking evaporate; she becomes awash in feeling and desperate in her attempts to establish any sort of connection with her partner. For Calvin, Jessica's strivings for union drive him even further away as he seeks a psychic haven in detachment.

TREATMENT

Conjoint therapy with a schizoid and histrionic is a challenge for any therapist. What the schizoid needs is antithetical to the histrionic; what the histrionic requires is what drives the schizoid to retreat. Through the dance of dual projective identification, we ascertain how one partner projects into the other the different aspects with which he identifies. Through identifying and understanding these projections, we can then begin to treat the abuse. The schizoid requires meticulous attunement to his variations in mood swings and the therapist must always anticipate them. The histrionic woman typically shows a tendency toward exhibitionism, displays clinginess and childlike attitudes in intimate relations, and is always threatening to leave. The therapist is met with such enactments as emotional outbursts, crying spells, temper tantrums, and competitive behaviors. To achieve some semblance of intimacy, she will behave provocatively and seductively or do anything to get a rise out of her nonresponsive partner. When frustrated by the schizoid partner, she will pound on him, get into competitive bouts, or, as a last resort, threaten him: "If you don't respond, I'm sure there are a lot of guys out there who will!"

What unites the couple is their dual projective identifications. The schizoid, who is inclined to be somewhat iconoclastic or unconventional, tends to isolate himself from society. But as he withdraws from his environment he begins to feel lonely and develops a yearning for some sense of relatedness. Not knowing how to connect in the normal sense he finds a person who becomes the receptacle for his projections. In spite of his loneliness, every effort the therapist makes toward expression of intimate feelings is met with marked resistance. The schizoid knows that while his defenses might provide him with an escape route from overwhelming involvement, his capacity for detachment ultimately interferes with his experience of relational closeness, satisfaction in his work, and sexual gratification. The histrionic knows that there are qualities within her that can be both alluring and repelling. She knows that she has experienced a lifelong pattern of deep yearnings that continue to go unmet. She has both the capacity and the willingness to reflect upon new ways of experiencing her emotionality, potentially leading to the fulfillment of her needs.

In the treatment, the therapist should be aware that the schizoid frequently develops symptoms of anxiety similar to those of claustrophobic patients. His defense in the therapy will be the same as that in his life—escape through detachment. The schizoid does not invite emotions; therefore, for the therapist to arouse emotions or attempt to bond prematurely will spell disaster as the schizoid inevitably re-experiences emotional engulfment.

In the initial phase of treatment, the schizoid will be content to "sit things out." The schizoid's role in the therapy at this point may be more as an observer than as a participant. This gives the therapist a perfect opportunity to connect with the histrionic, a connection the histrionic needs in order to pursue the therapeutic work, (similar to the suggestion of what to do with the borderline while the therapist bonds with the narcissist). The schizoid's "being there" may serve as an important transitional space for the therapist to focus primarily on the histrionic woman. Some therapists have argued that this may seem like a manipulation, but it really isn't because even if one member of the dyad continues, treatment is considered to be a success. The therapist "bathes" the histrionic with listening, containing, and empathic responses. With this psychic holding, the high-functioning histrionic woman will then be able to explore the many ways her intense affects and demands trigger even more withdrawal from the schizoid. First, the therapist must validate the histrionic's experience: "No, it's not just you. You are entitled to closeness, intimacy, passion, and of course all women have these yearnings. We all need intimacy, a sense that our desires and feelings count." Second, the histrionic may need extra individual sessions, increased therapeutic contact, such as the therapist accepting telephone calls.

It is at this juncture that the therapist can begin to bond with the schizoid, often by demonstrating a curiosity in his work. Schizoids are more likely to show interest if the therapist's interpretations are work related rather than object related. The schizoid may be more willing to consider how his detachment also provokes alienation in his co-workers, let alone his wife. For instance, the schizoid should be reminded of how his presecutory anxieties are linked with entrapment fantasies, exacerbating his tendency to withdraw from any intimacy. Though the therapist may not directly succeed in bonding with him, the interpretive work must lean toward helping the woman deal with his aggressive avoidance through the dual projective identifications. This will enhance the histrionic woman's understanding of how these unconscious barriers interfere with the real intimacy she craves.

In the second phase of treatment a delicate shift takes place. This phase involves the task of introducing schizoid and histrionic partners to their "internal abusers." The focus here is on each partner's participation in the "dance of emotional abuse," their dual projective identifications. The notion that the partners have remained unconsciously loyal to their internal abuser is foreign to them. The schizoid may reject the idea immediately in order to hold onto his anxiety of engulfment, without which he would have no need to flee. The histrionic may react to the therapist with "stranger anxiety," feeling suddenly that the therapist no longer understands her or is, in fact, betraying or wounding her.

The process is not a simple one. It is an exacting task, similar to the study of quarks, the search for subatomic pieces of the universal puzzle. Scientists describe the existence of top quarks as products resulting from protons and antiprotons. Because the speed of these tiny, colliding particles converts them directly into matter, the quarks end up being far heavier than the protons that produced them. Quarks serve as an apt metaphor for psychic processes: the enormous psychic energy required to produce and then maintain defenses may be greater than the very thing one needs to continue to defend against. Although originally our emotional experience may have put us at substantial risk, we finally reach a point when our defenses are not only obsolete but are obstacles in themselves.

If the therapist's interpretations prove to be premature, the therapist can return to a bonding period. This is a pivotal time for the therapy. The histrionic may see the schizoid enacting with the therapist what he does with her. The schizoid may be able to use the modeling provided by the therapist as she works with the histrionic. Eventually, though, the therapist needs to be bold, and deal with each partner's dynamics. It is better to work deeply and be somewhat "off" than to be superficial. The couch is not for either member of this couple. Eye contact, gazing, body language, all contribute to the therapist's ability to support each partner in understanding how his or her internal abuser functions and how this internal abuse gets played out in the couple's "dance." At this stage, treatment consists of weaning the couple away from the focus on the relationship to that of their own internal emotional development.

Similar to the woman with borderline or dependent personality disorder, the histrionic eventually learns she is not crazy or inappropriately needy. She gradually learns to disidentify with the schizoid's withdrawal, realizing that it is not a personal attack or assault against her but rather his defense against overwhelming anxieties about suffocation or engulfment. For the histrionic woman, the major task is to help her understand how her insistent demands and threats have the opposite effect of what she ultimately desires.

At this time in the therapy the schizoid patient will exhibit enjoyment at hearing correct interpretation and a willingness to work with his fantasies, and he may embrace dream work. He might even seek out individual analysis. As the histrionic sees these advancements, she too will be able to work at a deeper level, accessing the painful abandonment and rejection she experienced early in her life, which gets replicated in her current relationship. The exceptions to this are if the abuser is a severe schizoid, it is unlikely he will be able to remain in either the therapy or the relationship, and for the histrionic, once she no longer identifies with the schizoid's projections and is able to allow for the reality of his limitations for intimacy, she may choose to leave the relationship. However, if each partner is committed to the relationship and to the therapeutic work, then as the therapy progresses, the prognosis for the relationship improves.

‹❧ 8 ❧›

The Treatment
of Emotional Abuse

For the high-functioning woman, the delineation of emotional abuse is often difficult. With all her capabilities, her achievements and the accouterments of success, she is not viewed as an object of empathy. As the abuse she experiences becomes evident, she is judged. How could someone who is educated and accomplished allow herself to be abused? What's wrong with her?

In the theoretical and case material presented in these pages, it is clear that the more accurate questions to ask are: What went wrong in this woman's earliest life experience? How did parental failures influence her? How did she form the identifications she formed? How did she learn to get her needs met in some way and to some degree? In her high-functioning capacities, we look for the expression of her false self. In her intimate relationships, we see archaic needs and the replication of her earliest relationships. From these pages, we have also begun to understand in specific pairings (the narcissistic/ borderline couple, the borderline/narcissistic couple, the passive-aggressive/masochistic couple, the obsessive-compulsive/hysteric couple, and the schizoid/histrionic couple) what it takes for a clinician to treat the high-functioning abused woman and her partner. Now, let us examine some of the clinician's therapeutic functions and the phases of treatment.

THERAPEUTIC FUNCTIONS

Empathy

Empathy is both a mode of observation and the therapist's capacity to know the patient's experience. Kohut (1977) called it "vicarious introspection" (p. 303). There are three aspects to empathy. First, the therapist must listen with the "third ear"; in other words, as the patient reveals her manifest content, the therapist is listening for the meaning of that content, for what the patient is trying to express about her own experience as well as her experience with the therapist. What is the patient communicating to the clinician that is reminiscent of what she communicated as a child? How is the patient bringing to the therapist the experience she has in her everyday adult life? Second, through introspection, the therapist considers how this internal meaning is played out in the patient's current emotionally abusive relationship. At this point, the clinician will not usually verbalize what she comes to understand, but instead will use this understanding as the basis for her empathic responses. Third, the therapist offers empathic responses, which communicate to the patient that the therapist comprehends, both affectually and cognitively, the patient's emotional experience.

Almost without expectation, patients who are in emotionally abusive relationships have no words for the deepest meanings of their primitive experience. Since the foundation for the current abuse was laid in the early child–parent relationship, the affect involved was preverbal. Empathy not only creates a safe shared therapeutic space between patient and clinician, it also paves the way for putting words to the patient's most primitive existence.

Mirroring

Mirroring is a term devised by Kohut (1971, 1977), which describes the "gleam" in mother's eye reflecting her delight and participation in the child's healthy narcissistic/ exhibitionist displays, confirming the child's self-esteem. It is this maternal capacity to validate her child's inner life and value that enables the child to thrive and grow.

For the emotionally abused patient, mirroring is an essential therapeutic function that provides validation for her internal and external experience. Without such mirroring, the patient's original hurtful and compromising experience with the primary object(s) will be replicated. With such mirroring, the patient over time will come to trust in the therapeutic environment and will be able to comprehend her past life experience and how it is enacted in the present.

Containment

Containment is a term employed by Bion (1959, 1970) for a vital psychological function that the mother provides her infant. Bion believes this maternal function is available when the mother is in a state of reverie with her baby, a state in which she can receive her infant's affectual communication, filter it, and return it to the infant in a way the infant can utilize. Containment connotes the capacity for transformation of emotional experience into meaningful feelings and thoughts. This can occur only if the mother is able to sustain the infant's intolerable affects—for example, frustration and rage— long enough to decode or detoxify the painful feelings into a more digestible form.

Bion's conception of the container (mother/therapist) and the contained (infant/patient) is perhaps the most useful model with which the clinician can work. While empathic responses and mirroring offer connecting functions to the patient, it is only as the therapist is able to contain her patient's volatile, chaotic, and overwhelming affect that the affect can be used in the service of further emotional development. While each individual may require different therapeutic functions at different times during treatment, the containing function of the therapist is needed throughout the process. Narcissists need a preponderance of mirroring, certainly in the early phases of treatment. Borderlines are confused by empathic responses and may misperceive them as collusion or a lack of the boundaries they need so desperately. For borderlines, containment offers salvation. The therapist must be able to speak directly to the heart of their fragmentation. If the therapist cannot provide this containing function, the borderline will not be able to move beyond his or her primitive affectual states.

According to Grotstein (1981), the infant must experience the object as having taken in her projection and identified with it, so that it can be known and converted into a new experience. As the therapist uses her countertransference in the service of this process, s/he will be able to accept the patient's projections, identify with them long enough to comprehend their meaning, and return them to the patient transformed. For instance, if a patient does not show up for an appointment at a particularly pivotal time in the therapy, the therapist can examine her own countertransference reaction to this.

Does she feel worried, knowing that usually the patient is responsible and dependable in keeping her appointments? Might this mean that the patient is unconsciously giving the therapist her own experience of what it was like to wait for a mother who did not come? Perhaps the therapist finds herself feeling angry. Could the patient be offering the therapist her experience of the anger she felt, but could not express, at her parents' unavailability? To assume automatically that the patient is being resistant to treatment is to foreclose a deeper knowledge of the patient's experience.

Countertransference

The use of the therapist's countertransference is particularly important in treating emotional abuse. While it is essential that the therapist be able to detect when his or her unconscious material is negatively influencing the treatment, it is also true that there is enormous value for the patient in the therapist's ability to use his or her countertransference responses in the service of the patient and the treatment. Understanding the countertransference helps the therapist understand what should be interpreted and when. If acted out, unconscious countertransference reactions are harmful to the treatment. Instead, the countertransference must always be looked to as a wellspring of *information* for the therapist to use in understanding the patient's experience and to move the therapy forward in productive and transformative ways.

Let us look at a brief example. A domineering boyfriend has the abusive habit of verbally blasting his girlfriend each time she accuses him of changing plans at the last minute. In the treatment, this boyfriend began to display his abusive ways by canceling sessions just moments before they were to start. When he did come in for a session, he shouted at the therapist, "Just listen to what I have to say. If you say one word, I'm not coming back." At first, the therapist sat obediently in silence, listening to the patient's unremitting attacks against both her and the abused patient. After several such sessions, the therapist remembered how her strict mother would sometimes force her to sit in silence. By recognizing how trapped and paralyzed she felt, the therapist was able to use the information and avoid enacting it. She was able to shift out of her frozen state and respond to the abuser. She said: "I think you are letting me know what it felt like for you to have been whipped and brutalized by your father, how diminishing and paralyzing that was. Do you think this may be your way of helping me understand your helpless, little boy state?" The abuser experienced not rage but relief at being comprehended and contained. Despite some initial weak protests to the contrary, he was soon able to make use of the therapist's discussion of her countertransference experience in understanding his own enactments.

In this instance, it was vital to each partner of this couple for the therapist to rescue herself from her psychic entrapment. For the abused woman, it provided modeling; she could see how the therapist intervened with the abuse without escalating it. For the abuser, it opened a new therapeutic space, in which he could then begin to understand how he used attack and destruction both to ward off threats and to let the other know of his internal experience.

Couple Transference

The couple transference does for the couple what transference does for the individual, but is slightly more complex. Couple transference interpretations are derived from the analyst's experience and insights and are designed to produce a transformation within the dyadic relationship. To understand its complexity, I have integrated the notion of intersubjectivity, a well-known but confusing construct elaborated by many contemporary psychoanalysts. The couple transference refers to the mutual projections, delusions, and distortions, or shared couple fantasies, which become displaced onto the therapist. The notion of the "couple/therapist" transference opens up an entirely new therapeutic vista or transitional space in which to work. It is within this space that "real" issues come to life. It is the space wherein mutual projections, delusions, and distortions are displaced onto the therapist, and are fostered or joined by the therapist's imagination. For example, two spouses may share a collective couple fantasy that if they begin to depend upon the therapist, the therapist will "abuse" his/her authority and take advantage of them. Couples need to learn that dependency needs are normal, and when negated or severely denied, stir up fierce anxieties (persecutory, depressive, repressed).

THE THERAPIST AS SELFOBJECT

In his seminal work, Heinz Kohut (1971, 1977) develops the theory of self psychology, a developmental theory whereby the need for selfobjects is a lifelong goal. A selfobject function can be performed by a person or other agent (e.g., religion). We are all in need of good selfobjects as sources of validation and/or guidance. As the therapist furnishes essential selfobject functions for the patient—empathy, mirroring, and containment—the patient will make remarks about feeling better and stronger, having an improved sense of self, possibly without being able to understand why this progress has occurred. Listening, being there, and providing a frame and a therapeutic boundary, are therapeutic.

Failures on the part of the therapist are inevitable, even necessary, in order to address the patient's experience and as opportunities for a new, reparative experience. Provided that these failures are relatively minor (for example, *occasional* misunderstandings), they become opportunities for growth. And the patient will then achieve the ability to maintain selfobject functions within his or her own internal structure (Manfield 1992). As both partners in the conjoint therapy strengthen in their use of selfobject functions, they will be able to offer one another empathy, mirroring, and containment.

The Therapist as the Bonding and Weaning Object

Grotstein (1997) aptly refers to Klein and Kohut as the "odd couple" or as "secretly related." Kohut and Winnicott are of the bonding school and Klein is of the weaning school. We notice that Klein is more interested in the kind of mother the infant creates through his projections, distortions, and projective identifications. She claims that the infant is born with both oral libidinal and destructive sadistic impulses in relation to its objects (the "good breast" and the "bad breast"). Kohut reinforces the importance of the good mirroring selfobject. He emphasizes that bonding occurs through the reflection of the good caretakers who provide empathic responses that allow the child to bond to good selfobjects. When we think of the differences between Klein and Winnicott, we notice that Winnicott paid more attention to good-enough caretakers than did Klein. He offers us a different kind of mother than Kohut. Winnicott referred to a bonding mother, an environmental mother, a background mother, a being/doing mother, a containing/sustaining mother, a weaning mother. A good-enough mother–infant relationship translates in the therapy as a new relationship for the therapist–patient dyad that is, in and of itself, curative.

Winnicott claimed that his second marriage to Clare accounted for a major shift in his life. In Brett Kahr's book _The Life of Donald Winnicott_ (1996), the author writes:

> Without doubt, Clare Winnicott was a selfobject for her husband, as she stimulated and encouraged his creativity tremendously. Not surprisingly, Winnicott produced his most original and poignant papers during the time of his nineteen-year marriage to his second wife. Shortly after the couple met, Winnicott wrote to Clare, "Your effect on me is to make me keen and productive. This is all the more awful, because when I am cut off from you, I feel paralysed for all action and originality."

Winnicott offers us the valuable concept of _transitional space_ (1965). The transitional space permits two to be as one. It permits two to be as one. It permits a quality of experience ranging from being to doing, of moving between dependency and interdependency. In utilizing the therapist as a transitional object, the "abuse" can serve as a vehicle into health, by which I mean that as the therapist creates a facilitating environment, she uses her knowledge of the internal abusers each partner has carried forward from his or her early experience to understand and address the nature of the external abuse. In this way, she effects a new and transformative experience for the patients.

PHASES OF TREATMENT

The three phases of treatment delineated in this section are considered as preparatory work for more intensive individual psychotherapy or psychoanalysis. Each requires a profound capacity on the part of the therapist for containing. Specifically, the three treatment phases, each with its methods and goals, support effective treatment for both partners in emotionally abusive relationships.

Phase One: The State of Oneness

During the first phase of conjoint therapy it is rare that either partner shows much awareness of his or her inner life or the unconscious forces compelling it. There is a predominance of primitive defenses, accompanied by name-calling and stonewalling between victim and perpetrator. Each partner is in a state of fusion and collusion, whereby each lives emotionally inside the other. In this state of "oneness" the victim and aggressor are fused: there is little distinction between self and other. There is an intolerance for separateness. The aggressor feels justified in his or her acts. Neither the aggressor nor the victim sees how they both resort to splitting and projection to rid themselves of their unwanted parts or to rid the psyche of its intolerable affects.

The couple engages in dual projective identification within the therapy as well as in their everyday lives. It is the therapist's task in this first stage of treatment to provide each partner with the empathy and mirroring required to establish bonding and trust. In order to do this, the therapist must monitor his or her countertransference so as not to get caught up in blaming, or be pressured into deciding who is right and who is wrong.

In this initial stage of treatment, boundaries are established, helping to create a safe environment. To begin, a commitment is made between the therapist and the couple for at least eight sessions. This commitment and its follow-through will prevent the possibility of abandonment themes being acted out. It is in this phase that the idea of giving up the "quick fix" is introduced; the couple can begin to understand that emotional development is both a time and energy commitment.

As much as the therapist provides empathy and mirroring, s/he also incorporates into the containment a clear position on the abuse taking place. It is not too early for some preliminary interpretations to be offered, pointing out how abusive interactions occur when conflict arises. The therapist might say to the abuser, "If you feel vulnerable when you have a need, what you do is withdraw [or attack, as the case may be], because you fear rejection or because you cannot tolerate the possibility that your needs might not be met." This is the time to help both partners begin to assign names to their feelings and to their interactions.

It may be difficult for therapists who are trained psychoanalytically to offer managerial skills and communication techniques, but in the first stage of treatment such provision can be crucial. We need to educate the couple as to the difference between a criticism and a complaint.

Recognizing when one or both partners engage in openly expressing hostility is fairly easy, but being able to identify subtle forms of emotional abuse is more difficult for the fused couple. Belittling side comments, demeaning body language, whining, the use of sounds or noises to intimidate or cajole, not listening, mocking, cross-examining, imitating, repeating the partner, stonewalling—all these can be ways of causing intimidation or pain in the other. An abuser may not even realize that his teasing, "Have you met my spendthrift wife?" is a form of emotional abuse. Or that using irony and sarcasm (for instance, the husband who referred to his flat-chested wife as "Busty"), feels like a slap in the face. Such comments denigrate the other, just as does the wife who coyly asks her husband's boss at a cocktail party, "Are you going to reward my husband for being such a workaholic?"

The next step in this phase of treatment is for the therapist to help both partners find ways they would like the other to respond to them. The therapist's language can provide the couple, perhaps for the first time, with new tools for sharing their affective experience.

Phase Two: A State of Twoness

It is in this stage that the therapist introduces the partners to their internal abusers and to the notion of their dual projective identifications. It is also when the therapist becomes more actively involved in the couple transference. This is a hopeful stage accompanied by a burst of new energy and feelings of excitement. There is a gradual moving away from the "act of doing" to the "act of being," to thinking instead of acting out. Both abuser and abused begin to see that they each play a part in "the dance."

Discussion becomes possible about the previously unthinkable, the unknown, and the unspoken. There is more tolerance for ambiguity, a growing awareness of unconscious motivations and other compelling forces. It is the beginning of bonding with the therapist and separation from living emotionally "inside" the other and toward mutual interdependence. As the therapist emerges as a new selfobject, there is an opening of the therapeutic space (transitional space). This phase also has an educational component as the therapist suggests techniques to deal with aggression and submission (for example, "It's okay to fantasize about slamming a door in her face, but it's *not* okay to do it!").

Here, we examine the partners' dynamic processes, saying to the victim:

> When you get anxious you withdraw, you run away, you say things like, "I don't want to see you again." When you do that, you trigger abandonment anxieties in your partner; then you're not in a position to see what the real issues are about. Even so, he still has no right to verbally abuse you, but it is important for us to be aware of this interaction or the way the two of you "do the dance."

And to the abuser:

> When you get anxious, you attack, you assault, and become a tyrant. When you do this you evoke fear and panic in your partner. She then begins to withhold from you, withdrawing her affection, and you then become even more controlling [dual projective identification].

The therapist must support the growing capacity of the couple to contain their own affects and to begin to process them. Patients in this phase begin to feel safer and less anxious. But concurrently, because of this sense of safety, contact with dependency needs may increase, as will the dependency upon the therapist. The therapeutic space opens up further as the therapist is able to make provision for meeting some of those needs, perhaps allowing for extra sessions or telephone contact. It is at this time, too, that both the individual transferences and the couple transferences become stronger. The couple may still fight with one another, and even with the therapist, but there are clearer distinctions between self and other. We might see an interchange such as this vignette, reminiscent of young children struggling to be seen and heard:

"Let me tell you how I feel about your leaving the dishes in the sink last night."

"No! Let me tell you how I feel about your not answering me when I talk to you."

"I'm the one who brought up the issue about your leaving the dishes in the sink, and I'm the one who would like to discuss *this* with you. However, if you want to talk to me about my not answering you when you speak to me, believe me I promise you I will be more than happy to discuss my screw-up with you in a few minutes."

As the therapist protects the couple from mutual provocations and assaults within the neutral but compassionate therapeutic space, the partners find a certain

reliability in the therapist, which they then can use as
they take their first tentative steps toward being with one
another in new ways.

In addressing dual projective identifications, we begin to point out how the victim can serve as the perpetrator and the perpetrator serve as the victim. Both
partners begin to get a glimpse of their covert contribution to the abuse and to the defenses employed for the
sake of psychic safety. With this knowledge, the victim is
able to stand up to the abuse, and the perpetrator is able
to start intervening when s/he feels compelled to act out
the abuse.

Phase Three: Working Through—Becoming
Dependent and Interdependent

In this final phase, there is a new depth and richness to
the couple's experience, an awakening to the depressive
position where true reparation can take place. This phase
of treatment marks the beginning of a wish to repair the
damage, to embrace guilt, to express remorse and sadness, to heal the wounds and listen non-defensively to
one another's hurts. While old struggles may continue,
healthy dependency needs and the awareness of interdependence are budding. Each partner begins psychically to live outside the mental space of the other, as two
separate individuals united in a partnership. There is a

coming to terms with uncertainty, ambivalence, confusion, and dependency needs. There is a weaning away from the relationship to self-development. We begin to see a gradual diminution of repetitive negative projections along with a window of opportunity for further treatment (conjoint alongside concomitant individual psychodynamic therapy).

There is increased tolerance for guilt, mistakes, chaos, not knowing, and finding alternate ways to deal with frustration. There is less of a need to "spill over," to evacuate, and more capacity to wait and contain. Working through the couple transference, the victim develops insight in noting that she is not the sole target of aggression, for example, that the abuser does the same with "most women" (if the therapist happens to be a woman). In some instances, the victim develops enough ego strength to leave the relationship. The following are some interactions that occur in phase three. We might hear such exchanges as:

"Let's wait until later this afternoon before we decide."

"It would have been nicer if you could have told me you made other plans so I could have made some plans of my own."

"I don't think this is you talking, I think it's that barking dog inside of you."

"You can tell me whatever you wish. I am willing to hear what you have to say, but it is unacceptable for you to talk to me in that tone."

"You are so endearing when you talk to me like this. When you express your feelings, needs, and desires it makes me feel much closer to you. I can listen, and you don't have to attack me."

The movement from the Kleinian paranoid-schizoid position to the depressive position finds a parallel in Freud's developmental sequence of oral, anal, and genital; in Mahler's (1975) phases of separation-individuation; and in Kohut's transmuting internalization. In the depressive position the infant begins to see mother as a whole object with her own needs. There is space for reparation. As couples begin to face their real relationship instead of their fantasy relationship, there is an integration between ambivalence and conflict. There is more capacity to contain one's own sadness and loneliness as each partner takes more responsibility for his or her needs and actions.

There is also a working through of the couple transference. Like the "good-enough" mother, the therapist has allowed the psychic material to unfold (by not talking too much, doing too much, or wanting to cure), and is able to return to the patients the meaning and substance of their earliest relationships. Instead of abusing the therapist as they were abused, or as they abuse each other, they are now able to use the therapist/object as a reparation selfobject.

Exploring the dialectic (Hoffman 1994) between inner and external reality, clinicians are offered an extraordinary opportunity not only for discovery of the seeds of abuse but for a remarkable, transformative potential. Such treatment not only makes use of the therapist's empathy and containment capacities and her ability to use countertransference for productive means, but is enormously rewarding both for therapist and patients as abuse gives way to a healthy, interdependent relationship.

❧ 9 ❧

Techniques—A Final Word

Emotional abuse is a subtle phenomenon and a complex subject. In coming to terms with it, both patients and clinicians can experience great uncertainties, among them the issue of who is at fault. It has been my attempt in this book to show that both partners in an emotionally abusive relationship are perpetrators *and* victims because of the dynamics they share in their dual projective identifications. This is not to say, however, that abuse is to be tolerated as it is enacted between an abusive partner and his immediate victim.

High-functioning women are at particular risk, although the accouterments of their success might belie this assertion. Despite having many resources at their disposal through their education, professional accomplishments, and social standing, it is a bitter paradox that those very same resources serve to obfuscate the reality of emotional abuse. While these high-functioning women may be in unconscious collusion with their partners through their own psychic dynamics, it is clear they do not want or choose to be abused.

For any woman, including the high-functioning woman, it is time to learn that there is power in femininity. A woman does not need to repudiate her female identity to be strong. There is innate beauty and potency in the capacity to "know," to "feel," and to allow for her "vulnerability." A woman is perceptive, resourceful, clever. She has the ability to think, anticipate, and plan. These women have lived behind the veil of a false self, but it is through the courage to confront the failures of life's earliest relationships that they can repair them in the therapeutic work. It is only when the woman feels internally safe that she can give up the protective position of the false self and yield to the re-emergence of the true self. Such courage and repair occur in the safe therapeutic environment that we provide as clinicians—an environment in which the therapist understands the plight and psychodynamics of the emotionally abused woman.

TREATMENT POINTS AND TECHNIQUES

The following are some general guidelines for the therapist in dealing with the partners in an abusive relationship:

- See the couple together before transition into individual therapy in order to form a safe bond, and caution the partners not to move into individual work until the couple is ready (too early separation can induce a rapprochement crisis).
- Be aware that couple interaction can diminish individuality. Avoid such phrases as, "You *both* suffer from feelings of abandonment."
- Be aware that each partner experiences anxiety differently, and that these qualitative differences must be respected.
- The therapeutic alliance must be joined with the member who is more valuable, for example, the narcissistic abuser. (The tendency to flee/withdraw can pose a serious threat to treatment.)
- Do not be afraid to confront the abuse. Speak directly to the abuse with clear, definitive statements, while maintaining technical neutrality.
- Listen and be attentive. Maintain good eye contact and speak with meaning and conviction. Keep sentences short and cogent.
- Bond primarily with the healthy parts of both victim and perpetrator without losing sight of aggression, perversion, sadism, masochism, or victimization. We offer empathy to the vulnerability and the pain, but *not* to the aggression.
- When individual treatment occurs in conjunction with conjoint treatment, the same basic guidelines

apply. Privilege and confidentiality issues are still under the umbrella of conjoint treatment.

- Avoid asking too many questions and taking lengthy histories. Don't waste time! Start right in! The history and background information will automatically unfold within the therapy.
- Avoid technical terms. Simple explanations and interpretations are best. (The deeper the interpretation, the better. Better to be wrong and work deeper than to remain shallow and work perfunctorily.)
- Unravel the distortions by showing how both the abuser and victim confuse healthy needs with the fear of dependency.
- Use the patients' language to reflect their most intimate world. Provide "hostility free" language as alternatives to their current abusive language.
- Use your countertransference as a source of information. The more severely disturbed the patient, the more your countertransference is a resource.
- Work within the couple transference. It opens the therapeutic space and shows the couple how similar defenses occur with the therapist ("So it's not just me").
- Always keep in mind the "ideal" couple. This attitude sharpens your focus and safeguards you and the couple from getting lost within the "dance."

- Always re-evaluate the treatment goals and remind the couple why they entered treatment in the first place.

SUGGESTIONS FOR THE COUPLE

It may be necessary to educate our patients as well, to help them develop strategies and language with which to intervene with dual projective identifications. Some brief suggestions follow:

- State how you feel, even when the other person is not listening or even when you think "he will never change."
- Listen first, and wait for a quiet time to engage in conversation.
- Don't attack each other or get into battle or attacks. Don't allow your emotions to overwhelm you or indulge in an array of emotional hysterics. Instead, negotiate. "This is what I want and this is what I will do in exchange to get it." If you want sex, romance, money, or more time, negotiate for it. Remember to stay with what you need and present your story in a calm way.
- Don't leave the room angry. If a partner gets "heated up," reassure him or her that you will return in a short time when he/she calms down (be specific). Repeat if needed.

- Focus on remaining differentiated; don't get hooked into deception or manipulation. Recognize that you may have been manipulated. Tolerate feelings of helplessness or anger at being deceived until you know clearly what you want to say and do that will help to work it out
- One does not need to tell all (containment: no, you don't have to spill your guts or tell all).

In emotionally abusive relationships, couples express their pain by unconsciously repeating the dynamics and interactions they learned in their earliest life experiences. Up until the time that they enter treatment, they have been unable to profit from additional life experiences to any marked degree. The repetitive enactments of these couples can be seen in the light of lost wishes and dreams; they are merely strivings for a new experience in their interpersonal world. As clinicians, we need to be prepared to deal with the issues embedded in emotional abuse as our patient population seeks our help. Understanding the dance, the dual projective identification process, between the abuser and the abused dramatically enriches the therapeutic work and transcends both shame and blame, leading to new psychic development.

No woman deserves to be abused, physically, sexually, or emotionally. No one deserves to be undermined, mistreated, or violated. I have attempted to show that while all women, including high-functioning women, are not responsible for the abuse they experience, they are not helpless victims either. It is true that being in an emotionally abusive relationship can feel like being in a psychic war. But the goal is not to "win," "compete," or to destroy the "enemy." Rather, it is to learn how to honor needs, establish boundaries, and create a therapeutic transitional space in which two adults can experience each other in mutual respect and love. To this end, we need to remember that with each session, the opportunity for a new experience begins.

References

American Psychiatric Association (1994). *Desk Reference to the Diagnostic Criteria from DSM-IV*. Washington, DC: Author.

Bach, S. (1994). *The Language of Perversion and the Language of Love*. Northvale, NJ: Jason Aronson.

Bachman, R. (1994). *Violence against women, a national crime victimization survey report*. Los Angeles County Board of Supervisors Special Panel Report on Domestic Violence. Washington, DC: United States Department of Justice.

Bader, E., and Bader, P. P. (1988). *In Quest of the Mythical Mate*. New York: Brunner/Mazel.

Benjamin, J. (1988). *The Bonds of Love*. New York: Pantheon.

Berghold, J. (1991). The social trance: psychological obstacles to progress in history. *Journal of Psychohistory* 19(2):221–243.

Berton, P. (1994). Understanding Japanese negotiating behavior. *ISOP Intercom* 18(2):1–8.

Bion, W. (1959). *Experiences in Groups*. London: Tavistock.

——— (1962). *Learning from Experience*. New York: Basic Books.

——— (1967). *Second Thoughts: Selected Papers on Psycho-Analysis*. New York: Jason Aronson.

———— (1970). Attention and interpretation. In *Seven Servants*. London: Tavistock.

———— (1977). *Seven Servants: Four Works by Wilfred Bion*. New York: Jason Aronson.

Breuer, J., and Freud, S. (1893–1895). Studies on hysteria. *Standard Edition* 2.

Chasseguet-Smirgel, J. (1970). Feminine guilt and the Oedipus complex. In *Female Sexuality*. Ann Arbor: University of Michigan Press.

Curran, D. (1996). *Tyranny of the Spirit*. Northvale, NJ: Jason Aronson.

Dattilio, F., and Padesky, C. A. (1990). *Cognitive Therapy with Couples*. Sarasota, FL: Professional Resource Exchange.

DaVanzo, J., and Rahman, M. O. (1993). *American Families: Trends and Policy Issues*. Santa Monica, CA: Rand.

deMause, L. (1974). *The History of Childhood*. New York: Psychohistory Press.

———— (1991). The universality of incest. *Journal of Psychohistory* 19(2):123–164.

Dicks, H. (1967). *Marital Tensions: Clinical Studies toward a Psychological Theory of Interaction*. New York: Basic Books.

Doi, T. (1973). *The Anatomy of Dependence*. Tokyo: Kodansha.

Dorpat, T. (1993). The type C mode of communication—an interactional perspective. *International Journal of Communicative Psychoanalysis and Psychotherapy* 8:47–54.

Dutton, D. (1995). *The Domestic Assault of Women*. Vancouver: UCB Press.

Dutton, D., and Painter, S. L. (1981). Traumatic bonding: the development of emotional attachments in battered women and other relationships of intermittent abuse. *Victimology: An International Journal* 6:139–155.

Endleman, R. (1989). *Love and Sex in Twelve Cultures.* New York: Psychic Press.

Fairbairn, W. R. D. (1940). *Schizoid Factors in the Personality: An Object Relations Theory of the Personality.* New York: Basic Books, 1952.

Follingstad, D. R., Rutledge, L. L., Berg, B. J., et al. (1990). The role of emotional abuse in physically abusive relationships. *Journal of Family Violence* 5:107–120.

Freud, A. (1966). *The Ego and the Mechanisms of Defense,* revised edition. New York: International Universities Press, 1936.

Freud, S. (1914). On narcissism: an introduction. *Standard Edition.* 14:67–102.

———— (1915). Instincts and their vicissitudes. *Standard Edition* 14:109–140.

———— (1923). *The ego and the Id. Standard Edition* 19:1–66.

Gay, P. (1986). *Freud: A Life for Our Time.* New York: Norton.

Gilligan, C. (1982). *In a Different Voice: Psychological Theory and Women's Development.* Cambridge, MA: Harvard University Press.

Greenson, R. (1968). Disidentifying from the mother: its special importance for the boy. *International Journal of Psycho-Analysis* 49:370–374.

Grinberg, L. (1977). *Introduction to the Work of Bion.* New York: Jason Aronson.

Grotstein, J. (1981). *Splitting and Projective Identification.* New York: Jason Aronson.

———— (1990). Nothingness, meaninglessness, chaos, and the "black hole" III: the black hole. *Contemporary Psychoanalysis* 26(3):377–407.

——— (1997). *Klein and Kohut: an odd couple or secretly related?* The 20th Annual International Conference on the Psychology of the Self, Chicago, IL.

Grotstein, J., Lang, J. A., and Solomon, M. F. (1987). Convergence and controversy: II: Treatment of the borderline. In *The Borderline Patient*, vol. 2. Hillsdale, NJ: Analytic Press.

Grotstein, J., and Mason, A. (1996). Personal communication.

Guerin, P. J., Fay, L. F., Burden, S. L., and Kautoo, J. G. (1987). *The Evaluation and Treatment of Marital Conflict*. New York: Basic Books.

Hoffman, I. (1981). *Foundations of Family Therapy*. New York: Basic Books.

——— (1994). Dialectical thinking and therapeutic action in the psychoanalytic process. *Psychoanalytic Quarterly* 63(2):187–218.

Human Rights Watch. (1997). *The Human Rights Watch Global Report on Women's Human Rights*. New York: Human Rights Watch, August, pp. 1–13.

Iga, M. (1986). *The Thorn in the Chrysanthemum*. Berkeley, CA: University of California Press.

Johnson, F. (1994). *Dependency and Japanese Socialization: Psychoanalytic and Anthropological Investigations into Amae*. New York: New York University Press.

Kafka, F. (1971). The vulture. In *The Complete Stories*, pp. 442–443. New York: Schocken.

Kahr, B. (1996). *The Life of Donald Winnicott: A Biographical Portrait*. London: Karnac.

Kernberg, O. (1975). *Borderline Conditions and Pathological Narcissism*. New York: Jason Aronson.

——— (1990). Between conventionality and aggression: the boundaries of passion. Presented at the Cutting Edge Conference, University of California, San Diego, CA, April.

——— (1991a). Aggression and love in the relationship of the couple. *Journal of the American Psychoanalytic Association* 39:45–70.

——— (1991b). Sadomasochism, sexual excitement, and perversion. *Journal of the American Psychoanalytic Association* 39:333–362.

——— (1992). *Aggression in Perversity Disorders and Perversions.* New Haven: Yale University Press.

Klein, M. (1940). Mourning and its relation to manic-depressive states. In *Contributions to Psycho-Analysis, 1921–1945,* pp. 311–338. London: Hogarth, 1950.

——— (1948). *Contributions to Psycho-Analysis, 1921–1945.* London: Hogarth.

——— (1952). Notes on some schizoid mechanisms. In *Developments in Psychoanalysis,* ed. J. Riviere, pp. 242–321. London: Hogarth.

——— (1957). *Envy and Gratitude.* New York: Basic Books.

——— (1975). Love, guilt, and reparation. In *Love, Guilt, and Reparation and Other Works, 1921–1945,* ed. R. E. Money-Kyrle, pp. 306–343. New York: Free Press, 1937.

Kohut, H. (1971). *The Analysis of the Self.* New York: International Universities Press.

——— (1977). *The Restoration of the Self.* New York: International Universities Press.

Lachkar, J. (1983). The Arab-Israeli conflict: a psychoanalytic study. Doctoral dissertation. Los Angeles, CA: International College.

——— (1984). Narcissistic/borderline couples: a psychoanalytic perspective to family therapy. *International Journal of Family Psychiatry* 5(2):169–189.

——— (1992). *The Narcissistic/Borderline Couple: A Psychoanalytic Perspective on Marital Treatment.* New York: Brunner/Mazel.

——— (1993). Paradox of peace: folie à deux in marital and political relationships. *Journal of Psychohistory* 20(3):275–287.

——— (1997). Narcissistic/borderline couples: a psychodynamic approach to conjoint treatment. In *The Disordered Couple*, ed. L. Sperry and J. Carlson, pp. 259–284. New York: Brunner/Mazel.

Lansky, M. (1981). *Family Therapy and Major Psychopathology.* New York: Grune & Stratton.

——— (1987). Shame in the family relationships of borderline patients. In *The Borderline Patient*, vol. 2, ed. J. Grotstein et al., pp. 187–199. Hillsdale, NJ: Analytic Press.

——— (1995). The stepfather in Sophocles' *Electra*. In *Stepfathers*, ed. S. Cath, M. Shopper, and L. Tessman, pp. 1–33. Hillsdale, NJ: Analytic Press.

Lifton, R. (1986). *Nazi Doctors.* New York: Basic Books.

Loring, M. T. (1994). *Emotional Abuse.* New York: Lexington Books.

Mahler, M. S., Pine, F., and Bergman, A. (1975). *The Psychological Birth of the Human Infant: Symbiosis and Individuation.* New York: Basic Books.

Manfield, P. (1992). *Split Self/Split Object: Understanding and Treating Borderline, Narcissistic, and Schizoid Disorders.* Northvale, NJ: Jason Aronson.

Mason, A. (1981). The suffocating super-ego: psychotic break and claustrophobia. In *Do I Dare Disturb the Universe?*, ed. J. Grotstein, pp. 140–166. Beverly Hills, CA: Caesura.

——— (1994). *Quick Otto and Slow Leopold: The Freud–Fliess Relationship.* Los Angeles: Psychoanalytic Center of California.

Modell, A. (1976). The holding environment and the therapeutic action of psychoanalysis. *Journal of the American Psychoanalytic Association* 24:285–307.

Nakakuki, M. (1994). Normal and developmental aspects of masochism: transcultural and clinical implications. *Psychiatry: Interpersonal and Biological Processes* 57(3):244–257.

Painter, S. L. (1985). Why do battered women stay? Theoretical perspectives. *Highlights: Newsletter of the Canadian Psychological Association.* Old Chelsea, Quebec: Canadian Psychological Association.

Patai, R. (1983). *The Arab Mind.* New York: Scribner's.

Peace at Home, Inc. (1997). *Domestic Violence: The Facts.* Boston: Peace at Home, Inc.

Podell, R. M. (1992). *Contagious Emotions: Staying Well When Your Loved One Is Depressed.* New York: Pocket Books.

Richter, P. (1993). Clinton meets with human rights activists. *Los Angeles Times*, December 11, p. A10.

Robertson, D. (1995). Personal communication.

Rosenbaum, A., and O'Leary, K. (1981). Marital violence: characteristics of abusive couples. *Journal of Consulting and Clinical Psychology* 49:63–71.

Segal, H. (1967). *Introduction to the Work of Melanie Klein.* New York: Basic Books.

Sperry, L., and Maniaci, H. (1997). The histrionic-obsessive couple. In *The Disordered Couple*. New York: Brunner/ Mazel.

Stoller, R. (1975). *Sex and Gender*, vol 2. New York: Jason Aronson.

Stolorow, R., and Lachmann, F. (1980). *Psychoanalysis of Developmental Arrest: Theory and Treatment*. New York: International Universities Press.

Straus, M. A. (1980). Victims and aggressors in marital violence. *American Behavioral Scientist* 23(5):681–704.

Tustin, F. (1981). *Autistic States in Children*. London: Routledge & Kegan Paul.

Vaquer, F. (1991). An object relations approach to conflict and compromise. In *Conflict and Compromise: Therapeutic Considerations*, ed. S. Dowling, pp. 115–132. Monogram 7 of the Workshops Series of the American Psychoanalytic Association. Madison, CT: International Universities Press.

Walker, L. (1984a). *The Battered Woman Syndrome*. New York: Springer.

——— (1984b). Behavioral description of violence. In *The Battered Woman Syndrome*. New York: Springer.

Willi, J. (1982). *Couples in Collusion: The Unconscious Dimension in Partner Relationships*. Claremont, CA: Hunter House.

Winnicott, D. W. (1965). *The Maturational Processes and the Facilitating Environment*. New York: International Universities Press.

Wolberg, L. R. (1977). *The Technique of Psychotherapy*, third edition. New York: Grune & Stratton.

Index